HEALTHY HOMEMADE
Dog Treats

HEALTHY HOMEMADE
Dog Treats

MORE THAN 70 SIMPLE & DELICIOUS TREATS
FOR YOUR FURRY BEST FRIEND

SERENA FABER-NELSON

Skyhorse Publishing

Skyhorse Publishing books may be purchased in bulk at special discounts for sales promotion, corporate gifts, fund-raising, or educational purposes. Special editions can also be created to specifications. For details, contact the Special Sales Department, Skyhorse Publishing, 307 West 36th Street, 11th Floor, New York, NY 10018 or info@skyhorsepublishing.com.

Skyhorse® and Skyhorse Publishing® are registered trademarks of Skyhorse Publishing, Inc.®, a Delaware corporation.

Visit our website at www.skyhorsepublishing.com.

10 9 8

Library of Congress Cataloging-in-Publication Data

Names: Faber-Nelson, Serena, author.
Title: Healthy homemade dog treats: more than 70 simple, delicious &
    nourishing recipes for your furry best friend / by Serena Faber-Nelson.
Description: New York, NY: Skyhorse Publishing, [2019]
Identifiers: LCCN 2019006606| ISBN 9781510744714 (hardcover: alk. paper) |
    ISBN 9781510744738 (ebook)
Subjects: LCSH: Dogs—Food—Recipes. | Dogs—Nutrition.
Classification: LCC SF427.4 .F34 2019 | DDC 636.7/083—dc23 LC record available at
    https://lccn.loc.gov/2019006606

Cover design by Daniel Brount
Cover photo by Alexander Mayes Photography

Print ISBN: 978-1-5107-4471-4
Ebook ISBN: 978-1-5107-4473-8

Printed in China

Disclaimer: The author and publisher will not be held liable for the use or misuse of the information in this book. Before making any changes or additions to your dog's diet, remember to check with your local vet regarding your dog's nutritional needs.

For Soda.

CONTENTS

WELCOME

I'm unbelievably excited to welcome you to my first book—*Healthy Homemade Dog Treats*. Or as I like to call it—your modern dog treat bible.

If you've bought this book, I know you love your dog. I know you want to have more control about what exactly goes into their diet. I know you want to look after your furry best friend the best way you can.

Yet, in my years of expert research and kitchen experiments, I've discovered the biggest roadblock for dog owners in making their own dog treats is the recipes themselves.

If you're faced with a dog treat recipe that calls for ten obscure ingredients, requires forty minutes prep, and still ends up looking like a brown, crumbly mess—you're reaching for that expensive bag of ready-made dog treats faster than I can say "fetch." And I'm with you—I'd much prefer to be snuggling on my couch with my pupper, binge watching Netflix, than wasting hours in the kitchen cooking some treat my dog barely cares about.

So of course, when I was writing this book I knew the recipes had to be tasty and healthy for our pups, quick and easy for us to make, and finally, useful in our everyday lives.

We're dog owners—we want treats our dog can happily chew on while we head out to work, yummy high-value training treats that gets results, or treat-ball fillers that keep their attention for longer. We want simple, we want easy, we want delicious.

That's why this book is based around quick, easy, everyday recipes that deliver beautiful, snackable results.

Unlike many other dog recipe books, the dog treat recipes in this book focus on all natural, nourishing, human-grade ingredients. Many recipes share staple ingredients that can be found at your local supermarket, easy to follow cooking methods, and use basic equipment found in any kitchen. The end results are healthy treats that look so good you'll want to eat them yourself.

With an allergy alternatives guide, easy read buttons for Dairy Free, Grain Free, and Vegetarian dog treat recipes, I've made it so you can see what's in each treat at a quick glance. Recipes that can be made in less than fifteen minutes also have a special icon (because who doesn't love things quick and easy?). Breakout boxes highlight the benefits of ingredients (did you know raspberries are an excellent source of fiber for dogs?). And because I know we all love to celebrate with our doggos, there's a whole section dedicated to special occasions such as birthdays and holidays.

Every single recipe in this book is suitable for a beginner treat maker. Just pick your favorite to start and keep going (after reading all the important health and produce notes in the beginning chapters, of course!).

I'd encourage you all, once you master the recipes in this book, to start experimenting with your own creations (always checking with your vet first!) and have fun with the treat making process. Your dog will love you for it.

Now go forth and Treat Yo' Dog!

—Serena xx
www.prettyfluffy.com

WHY DO WE GIVE DOG TREATS?

When it came to writing this book the most important message I wanted to convey was *why* we give treats to dogs, and how treats form an integral part of the bond between owner and dog. Let's take a closer look at just why we give our dogs treats.

Treats for Training

It's widely recognized that using treats in positive reinforcement training is the kindest and most effective form of training for dogs around the world. When presented with a treat, a dog's attention will become instantly sharper and focused—making results happen swiftly.

Treats for Distraction

Whether it's a piece of jerky to chew, or a treat ball filled with goodies, treats are a great way to distract your dog in a positive way. For dogs that are left alone, or suffer from separation anxiety, treats are a great way to keep them distracted while you're gone. Or maybe you're at home and just need your dog's attention diverted while you finish an important task. Regardless, it's treats for the win, every time.

Treats for Bonding

While it may not be as practical as training treats, or as useful as distraction treats, giving your dog a treat "just because" it a totally valid reason in it's own right. Treating your dog with the odd dog biscuit is a great way to strengthen the bond between the two of you. Your dog associates the reward with the person dispensing the treat, building trust and affection. It's also a great way for new faces in a household to earn a dog's loyalty! Never underestimate the power of the humble dog treat.

Treats for Celebrating

Last but certainly not least, we love to pamper our dogs with treats when we're celebrating. Maybe it's a tenth birthday, a happy Gotcha Day, or we want to tell our dog how much we love them on Valentine's Day. Whatever the cause for celebration, treats are a great way to show your dog they're an important part of the family.

WHY MAKE HOMEMADE TREATS?

The Ingredients.
You know exactly what's in them—no hidden preservatives or nasties.

The Process.
They're made by you, in your kitchen, and there's no fear of scary recalls.

The Cost.
Homemade treats are much cheaper than store-bought alternatives. For the cost of one bag of store-bought treats, you can make up to five times the homemade treats.

The Flavor.
You get to experiment with flavor combinations that store-bought treats don't offer—including nourishing superfoods and your dog's favorite ingredients.

The Experience.
Making your own dog treats allows you to hone your cooking skills, and makes you aware of alternative ingredients you may not have used before. If you have kids, it's also a great way to get them involved in learning simple recipes and the rewarding experience of looking after the family pet.

The Love.
By making something especially for your dog, you show them just how much you care.

Treats should never make up more than 10% of your dog's diet. While giving your dog treats is a positive act, overfeeding is not. Some of these recipes make large quantities, so consider freezing some, or sharing with doggie friends—you'll have the most popular dog at the park!

THE PANTRY

While some treats call for special ingredients and equipment, with these staples you should find yourself ready and able to whip up a batch of treats at a moment's notice.

STAPLE PANTRY INGREDIENTS:

Whole wheat flour
Rice flour
Almond flour
Coconut flour
Rolled oats
Honey
Organic peanut butter
Eggs
Plain organic yogurt
Carob drops

EQUIPMENT:

High quality kitchen knife
Large chopping board
Peeler
Colander/strainer
Measuring cups and spoons
Mixing bowls
Mixing spoons
Spatula
Whisk
Baking trays/pans
Baking racks
Rolling pin
Assorted cookie cutters (dog bone essential!)
Pastry brush
Piping bag/s (or Ziploc bags)
Airtight containers for storage
Ice cube trays and/or popsicle molds
Aluminum foil
Baking paper

BIG TICKET ITEMS:

Blender or food processor
Stand mixer (not a necessity but it makes things a lot easier!)
Ice cream maker

HEALTHY ALLERGY ALTERNATIVES

While most of the treats in this book are allergy friendly, here are some handy alternatives for pooches with special dietary needs. Experiment with the below options to see which ones your dog loves the most. Remember to always check with your vet before introducing new foods into their diet.

EGGS
- Simmer ¼ cup of flax seed meal in ¾ cup of water for 5–7 minutes, or until thick. Use 4 tablespoons for 1 egg.
- Add 1 tablespoon of chia seeds to 3 tablespoons of water. Let sit for 10 minutes to form a gel to replace 1 egg.
- 1 ripe banana, mashed, replaces 1 egg.
- 1 tablespoon of unsweetened applesauce replaces 1 egg.

MILK
- Unsweetened coconut milk
- Unsweetened almond milk

WHEAT & GLUTEN
- Almond flour
- Coconut flour
- Flaxseed meal
- Rice flour

Note: Make your own flour alternative by combining a mixture of the above flours.

YOGURT
- Coconut milk yogurt
- Almond milk yogurt

BUTTER
- Coconut oil

DOG-FRIENDLY FRUIT & VEGETABLE SEASONAL GUIDE

Buying seasonal produce not only makes your shopping budget go further, but it means you're always getting the freshest, tastiest produce out there.

When fruits and vegetables are in abundant local supply they will be lower in price, and the journey from farm to plate will be much shorter, meaning you get the produce at the peak of it's quality.

I've rounded up a general guide of my favorite dog-safe seasonal fruits and vegetables to have you making your own fresh treats in no time.

	FRUIT	VEGETABLES
SUMMER	bananas blackberries blueberries cantaloupe/rockmelon mango pineapple raspberries strawberries watermelon	peppers carrot celery cucumber green beans potato (always cooked, never raw or green) zucchini
AUTUMN	apples blackberries bananas cantaloupe/rockmelon cranberries honeydew kiwi mango pears pomegranate raspberries strawberries	broccoli peppers carrot cauliflower cucumber green beans parsnip potato (always cooked, never raw or green) pumpkin sweet potato (always cooked) zucchini
WINTER	apples bananas kiwi pears pineapple	broccoli broccolini carrot cauliflower kale parsnip potato (always cooked, never raw or green) pumpkin sweet potato (always cooked)
SPRING	bananas blueberries cantaloupe/rockmelon kiwi mango pineapple strawberries watermelon	broccoli peppers cauliflower celery cucumber green beans parsnip peas potato (always cooked, never raw or green) pumpkin sweet potato (always cooked)

Important Note: Your geographic location does affect the seasonality of produce. Check online for up-to-date information if you're after a specific area seasonality produce guide.

CHARTS & CONVERSIONS

OVEN TEMPERATURES

Description	Very cool	?	Cool	?	Very moderate	Moderate	?	Moderately Hot	Hot	?	Very Hot
Fahrenheit	225	250	275	300	325	350	375	400	425	450	475
Celsius	105	120	130	150	165	180	190	200	220	230	242

WEIGHTS

Ounces	Grams
1	25
2	50
3	75
4	110
5	150
6	175
7	200
8	225
9	250
10	275
11	315
12	350
13	365
14	400
15	425
16/1lb	450

VOLUMES

Fluid Ounces	Milliliters
1	25
2	55
3	75
4	120
5	150
6	15
7	200
8	225
9	250
10	275
15	425
20/1 pint	570
1¼ pints	725
1½ pints	850
1¾ pints	1 Liter

A HANDY GUIDE TO BUYING ORGANIC

There's never been a better time than now for you and your pooch to go organic.

Growing research indicates that organic produce is superior in vitamins, minerals, nutritional content—and of course, taste! Organic farming methods are kinder to our planet while producing high quality fruit and vegetables free from harmful pesticides and artificial additives.

Yet buying organic produce can be expensive, so if you can't switch over entirely, here's a handy cheat sheet on the foods most contaminated (commonly known as the "Dirty Dozen") and those that are less affected by pesticides (the "Clean Fifteen").

For the recipes in this book, I have specifically not labeled fresh ingredients as organic/non-organic, yet where possible, I'd always recommend buying the organic version—for the health of you, your dog, and the planet.

Important Note: These lists feature some foods that are toxic for dogs. Use them as an organic reference guide only.

The Dirty Dozen (in order of contamination)	The Clean Fifteen (in order of least contamination)
Apples	Onions
Celery	Corn
Sweet bell peppers	Pineapples
Peaches	Avocado
Strawberries	Cabbage
Nectarines	Peas
Grapes	Asparagus
Spinach/kale/collard greens	Mangoes
Lettuce	Eggplant
Cucumbers	Kiwi
Blueberries	Rockmelon/cantaloupe
Potatoes	Sweet potatoes
	Grapefruit
	Watermelon
	Mushrooms

WHAT ARE DOG-SAFE FOODS?

All the recipes in this book have been made and tested using dog-safe ingredients. However, before introducing any new foods into your dog's diet, please *always* check with your vet.

Just like us, certain dogs can react to different foods. They also have much smaller bodies and therefore digest and process foods differently. Smaller breeds only have a few kilos body weight to process their food. When feeding your dog a new food it's important to observe them to make sure they don't have any reactions.

If your dog has pre-existing health issues or intolerances, is smaller than average, or is in ill health, it is even more imperative to be vigilant and check with professionals before changing your dog's diet in any way.

Important Ingredient Notes

Almonds
Almond flour is used in a variety of recipes within this book and is classified as a food safe for dogs. However, due to the high fat content in almonds, it's best to feed recipes with almond flour in small amounts.

Baking Soda
This leavening agent is used in a handful of recipes in this book, as it is a chemical agent that helps batter rise when baked. It is widely observed that baking soda, while harmful if fed directly to your dog, is safe to use within recipes where it is diluted by other liquids and ingredients. To stay on the safe side, always limit treats containing leavening agents to just 1–2 daily (less for smaller breeds). If you or your vet have concerns about using leavening agents in a dog treat recipe, it's best to leave it out. The treat will not rise, and therefore be less fluffy and more dense, but will taste just as good.

Yogurt
When using yogurt in recipes always ensure you choose organic, natural, plain yogurts. Yogurts with artificial sweeteners and added sugars are not recommended for dogs.

Keep in mind, like humans, some dogs are lactose intolerant.

Peanut Butter

For many dog owners around the globe, peanut butter is a go-to treat—and for this reason it's included in many of our recipes. However it's important to always choose organic, natural peanut butters. And beware of any peanut butter with the ingredient "Xylitol." Xylitol is a sweetener that is toxic to dogs and should be avoided.

Coconut Oil

The darling of the health food set, this ingredient also reports a myriad of benefits for dogs. It's a great substitute for a number of traditional baking ingredients and for that reason has been used widely in this book. However, it should be noted that coconut oil is also high in fat and should always be consumed in moderation. This is especially important if your dog is heavily overweight or prone to pancreatitis.

Sugars

Foods containing processed sugars are an absolute no-no for dogs. Natural based sugars, such as maple syrup and honey can be consumed in moderation. You should still limit serving sizes to protect your dog's overall health and waistline. If you or your vet have concerns about your dog's sugar consumption, you can leave these ingredients out (when it's just a tablespoon or so) or replace with a sugar alternative—such as ripe mashed banana.

WHAT IS XYLITOL?
Xylitol is a sugar substitute used in many human foods—from sugar-free gum and candy to baked goods. It is also extremely toxic to dogs. Ensure that any products containing xylitol are always safely out of reach of your dog. For foods such as peanut butter, always check the label to make sure they contain no xylitol.

FOODS TO AVOID

The following human foods are toxic to dogs and should be avoided at all times:

Alcohol
Apple seeds
Avocado
Cacao powder
Caffeinated foods and beverages
Cherries
Chocolate (all variations)
Coffee
Citrus fruits
Fat trimmings
Garlic
Grapes
Macadamia nuts
Mushrooms
Nutmeg
Onions (including chives)
Potato leaves and stems
Raisins
Rhubarb leaves
Salt
Stone fruit pits (i.e., apricots, mangoes, etc.)
Tomato leaves and stems
Xylitol (used in peanut butter, gum, and candy)
Yeast dough

FURTHER NOTES FOR THE READER

Ingredient Notes

- All eggs used in this book are free range.
- All meats used here are free range with no added hormones.
- Always wash all fruit and vegetables thoroughly under cold running water before preparing.

Method Notes

- If the recipe calls for melted coconut oil, melt it over a low heat on the stove. Do not melt coconut oil in the microwave.
- If your biscuit dough becomes too dry and crumbly, spray sparingly with water to improve the consistency. If it becomes too sticky, a tablespoon of coconut flour should help (this is more drying than other alternative flours).
- Practice makes perfect. The ingredients used to make dog treats can be harder to manipulate than standard treats made of butter and sugar. Just remember, all your dog cares about is the fantastic taste!
- Never refreeze thawed treats. It can change the texture and consistency of treats, which can make them messy, crumbly, and separated.

Icon Legend

Grain Free   Dairy Free   Vegetarian

 Make in less than 15 minutes (excludes refrigeration/freezing time).

No-Bake Treats

No-bake dog treats really are the best place to start when making your own dog treats. These recipes require no fancy baking techniques; take mere minutes of your time to make, and the best part? You don't even have to turn on your oven.

If you're just getting started with making your own dog treats, these are the best ones to make first. They allow you to become familiar with some of the main ingredients used with dog treats that are not commonly used in regular everyday baking and cooking.

All the recipes make small batches so it's not too devastating if you make a mistake. Most can be made in less than ten minutes (with extra time for refrigeration or freezing), which also frees up more time for playtime with your pup!

HANDY HINT: *Use a gentle pressure when rolling the balls. The mixture can be sticky and heavy handedness can cause it to crumble.*

NO-BAKE PEANUT BUTTER BALLS

—————— MAKES 25–30 TREAT BALLS. ——————

This recipe was one of the first dog treat recipes I ever developed. It's so simple and easy, it's a great one to do with kids and get them in on the fun. You can literally have these babies ready to go into the fridge within 5 minutes.

½ cup plain organic yogurt
1 cup organic peanut butter
2½ cups rolled oats

1. Line a flat baking tray with baking paper.

2. Mix the yogurt and peanut butter until it forms a paste.

3. Add the oats ½ cup at a time, ensuring they are fully coated and no dry spots form. You will be left with a heavy mixture.

4. Scoop out bite-sized pieces with a spoon and roll into little balls.

5. Place on the lined tray, refrigerate for 1 hour, and serve.

PEANUT BUTTER: *A tasty source of protein used to build and repair muscle tissue, peanut butter is filled with good fats that support a healthy cardiovascular system.*

CRANBERRY ENERGY BITES

———————————— MAKES 15–20 ENERGY BITES. ————————————

While these energy bites may not be as beautiful as their coconut-covered bliss ball cousins (Coconut Bombs, page 33), they get two paws up for flavor. With a stickier consistency than most edible treat balls, they make a great Kong stuffer as well.

⅓ cup dried cranberries
1 cup almond flour
⅓ cup organic peanut butter

1. Line a flat baking tray with baking paper.

2. Add all ingredients to food processor and mix until smooth.

3. Scoop out bite-sized pieces with a spoon and roll into little balls.

4. Place on the lined tray, refrigerate for 30 minutes, and serve.

CRANBERRIES: *Cranberries are rich in antioxidants and nutrients that help support a healthy immune system in dogs. Always feed in moderation as too many can cause an upset stomach.*

BROWNIE POPS

MAKES APPROXIMATELY 15 BROWNIE POPS.

While chocolate treats are a definite no-no for dogs, this sweet carob treat is as close to the real deal as you can get. They make a great addition to puppy parties, and I've even seen some dogs' humans sneak a few when they think no one is looking!

2 cups plain air-popped popcorn
1 tablespoon carob powder
2 tablespoons honey
1 teaspoon water
¼ cup organic peanut butter

HANDY HINT: *To air pop your popcorn, simply pour plain kernels into a brown paper lunch bag, fold over the top of the bag twice to seal it closed, and microwave for 1½ minutes, or until the popping slows.*

1. Line a flat baking tray with baking paper.

2. Place popcorn into paper bag and crush with rolling pin. Ensure all kernels are popped fully and any uncooked kernels are removed.

3. Combine carob powder, honey, water, and peanut butter in bowl. Add crushed popcorn and mix until well combined.

4. Scoop out bite-sized pieces with a spoon and roll into little balls. Place on the lined tray. Refrigerate for one hour to chill, then serve.

BANANA & BEET BITES

———— MAKES 12–15 TREAT BITES. ————

Perfectly pink and chock-full of flavor, these are some of the quickest, healthiest dog bliss balls you can make. I usually prefer to serve them "naked" but if your dog goes coconuts for coconuts, the optional coating will go down a treat.

¼ cup grated beetroot
1 small banana (peeled and roughly chopped)
1 cup almond flour
⅓ cup unsweetened finely shredded coconut

1. Add all ingredients to food processor and mix until smooth.

2. Scoop out bite sized pieces with a spoon and roll into little balls.

3. *Optional*: Toss each ball gently in finely shredded coconut until well coated.

4. Place on a flat tray lined with baking paper, refrigerate for 30 minutes, and serve.

HANDY HINT: *You can choose any type of apple for your Edible Kong; however, Granny Smith varieties have the lowest amount of natural sugar.*

EDIBLE KONG

———————— MAKES 1 EDIBLE KONG. ————————

Now, even though this technically could be called "instructions" more than a recipe, it's too ingenious not to include. With just two ingredients and two steps, it's possibly the easiest dog treat recipe known to man. Oh—and it will keep your dog entertained for ages.

1 small organic Granny Smith apple
Organic peanut butter for the filling
   or try our Perfect Peanut Butter Filling
   (page 43)

1. Wash, core, and remove any stickers from your apple. It's important to ensure the apple is fully cored as apple seeds contain cyanide and should not be consumed by dogs.

2. Stuff the core with your desired filling and serve.

HANDY HINT: *If you want a crispier version of the bars, use fewer carrots as they have a high water content.*

CARROT CAKE TREAT BARS

—————— MAKES 12 CARROT CAKE BARS. ——————

When coming up with this recipe, I originally intended to make carrot cake balls. But the more I tested, I knew bars were the real winner. The added bonus is that you can slice the bars as small as you want and turn them into excellent training treats.

7 Medjool dates (pitted)
4 medium carrots
1 teaspoon cinnamon
3 cups rolled oats

1. Lightly grease an 8 x 8" pan.

2. Place dates in a bowl and cover with boiling water. Allow to stand for 5 minutes to soften, then drain.

3. While the dates are soaking, finely grate your carrots (either in a food processor or by hand).

4. Add all ingredients to food processor and process until well combined.

5. Press the mixture firmly into the greased pan—it should be approximately ¾-inch thickness.

6. Refrigerate for a minimum of 2 hours to set.

7. Slice into bars and serve.

DATES: *Dates are low in fat and high in fiber and make a great sweet addition in recipes. However, their high sugar content means they should be used sparingly in your dog's diet.*

HANDY HINT: *If the mixture is too dry or wet, simply add extra oats or coconut oil to correct.*

COCONUT BOMBS

─────── **MAKES 16 TREAT BALLS.** ───────

These treats are so yummy that they often go missing from the fridge in our house—the fresh flavor combination is a crowd favorite! Like most of our no-bake treats, these Coconut Bombs take mere minutes to make and only 30 more to set.

⅓ cup coconut oil
2–3 tablespoons organic peanut butter
2 cups rolled oats
⅓ cup unsweetened shredded coconut

1. Add coconut oil, peanut butter, and rolled oats to food processor and mix until well combined.

2. Scoop out bite-sized pieces with a spoon and roll into little balls.

3. Toss each ball gently in the finely shredded coconut until well coated.

4. Place on a flat tray lined with baking paper, refrigerate for 30 minutes, and serve.

COCONUT: *The good fats in coconuts mimic the properties of antioxidants and boost vitamin E, promoting tissue health and shiny coats.*

DOGGYLATO

There's no better frozen fun for your Fido than these "Doggylato" ice cream blends. I tend to make them in smaller quantities, as they don't freeze long-term as well as full-fat ice cream for humans. Served up as a summer's day treat or frozen in a Kong, your dog will be begging for more. Once you master the below combinations, I encourage you to get creative with your own dog-safe ice cream combos!

Ice cream maker required.

RASPBERRY RIPPLE

½ cup fresh raspberries
1 teaspoon pure maple syrup
1 cup plain organic yogurt

1. Place raspberries and maple syrup in blender or food processor and pulse until they form a puree.

2. Stir yogurt into the puree.

3. Place the mixture into ice cream maker and let mix until thickened, about 15–25 minutes.

4. Remove and serve.

PEANUT BUTTER & BACON

1 cup plain organic yogurt
½ cup organic peanut butter
⅓ cup Pup-Friendly Coconut Bacon (page 45)

1. Place yogurt and peanut butter in blender or food processor and pulse until they are well combined.

2. Stir in the Pup-Friendly Coconut Bacon.

3. Place the mixture into ice cream maker, and let mix until thickened, about 15–25 minutes

4. Remove and serve.

BANANA

1 cup plain organic yogurt
1 banana
1 teaspoon honey

1. Place all ingredients in blender or food processor and pulse until they are well combined.

2. Place the mixture into ice cream maker, and let mix until thickened, about 15–25 minutes.

3. Remove and serve.

STRAWBERRY

8 large fresh strawberries
1 teaspoon honey
1 cup plain organic yogurt

1. Hull strawberries and cut into quarters.

2. Place strawberries and honey in blender or food processor and pulse until they form a puree.

3. Stir yogurt into the puree.

4. Place the mixture into ice cream maker, and let mix until thickened, about 15–25 minutes.

5. Remove and serve.

YOGURT: *A good source of calcium and protein for dogs, the bacteria in yogurt promotes a healthy digestive system. Always opt for natural, organic varieties.*

PUP-SICLES

—————————— MAKES 6 PUPSICLES. ——————————

These pup-sicles are fun to make, and are so versatile. Serve them up in traditional popsicle molds (carrot sticks make an excellent "popsicle stick"), freeze the mix into Kongs directly, or add to ice cube trays for a smaller reward. A refreshing treat for a hot summer's day.

3 cups plain organic yogurt
1 cup fresh fruit—choose from the following
    dog-safe fruits: blueberries, raspberries,
    strawberries, mango, pineapple,
    watermelon, or cantaloupe.

Popsicle molds or ice cube trays required.

> **HANDY HINT:** *To make a version for yourself, add 3 tablespoons sugar and a dash of lemon juice to the recipe!*

1. Combine 1½ cups yogurt and 1 cup fruit in blender or food processor to form a smoothie.

2. Pour into your popsicle molds, alternating between the smoothie mix and spoonfuls of the remaining plain yogurt.

3. Place in the freezer for 6 hours or until frozen solid.

4. Slide out each popsicle to serve. For easy removal, run the molds under warm water for a few seconds.

MANGO: *As well as being a tasty treat, the natural enzymes in mangoes have been shown to help dogs with arthritis.*

Kong & Treat Ball Stuffers

Kongs and treat balls are brilliant interactive toys that provide mental and physical stimulation for dogs and help keep them entertained for long periods of time. The unique cone shape of the Kong, with its hollowed-out center, allows you to stuff it with all sort of fillings—and your dog has hours of fun trying to get it out!

Treat balls, on the other hand, work best with dry fillings. Simply empty your treats into the ball and the puzzle releases treats as your dog moves the ball around.

When first stuffing your Kong or treat ball, it's important to make it easy for your dog. For treat balls, ensure it's set to its easiest setting, and manually show your dog how to move the ball to get the treats to fall out. With a Kong, put a small amount of your filling at the top opening. Your dog will be easily able to lick the filling out without too much work, and experience the reward of their tasty treat.

You don't want to overfill your Kong at the start, as your dog may give up! The easier you make his initial Kong experience the more inclined he'll be to stick at it when the treat is harder to get.

As your dog becomes more confident, start to push the filling further into the bottom of the Kong, making your pupper work harder for their reward. Before long you'll be able to start layering your treats and freezing your Kong for a greater challenge.

PERFECT PEANUT BUTTER FILLING

---------- FILLS ONE KONG OR HOLLOW UNCOOKED BONE. ----------

This peanut butter filling really is too perfect. Its thick consistency makes it much easier for filling and it's a great alternative to expensive store-bought fillings. The added bonus is you know exactly what's in it! Simply mix up and pop into your dog's favorite Kong or raw bone. Remember, never feed your dogs cooked bones and always supervise them when feeding any bones.

---

3 parts organic peanut butter or almond butter
1 part coconut flour
(Measure ingredients to fit your Kong or bone size)

> **HANDY HINT:** *Be sure not to use too much flour in your mixture as this could cause it to lose its smooth consistency and become crumbly.*

1. Combine ingredients in a small bowl and stir together until you don't see the flour. If you feel it is still too runny, add a little more coconut flour.

2. Take a spoon or icing knife and smooth it into your Kong or dog bone until it is tightly compact.

3. Serve immediately at room temperature or freeze until solid.

HANDY HINT: *Avoid feeding human recipes for Coconut Bacon to dogs. They contain a number of ingredients that are not safe for your pupper.*

PUP-FRIENDLY COCONUT BACON

—————— FILLS APPROXIMATELY 3 KONGS, OR CAN BE SERVED INDIVIDUALLY. ——————

Coconut Bacon for humans almost has a cult following now, with it's crunchy bacon-like texture and taste—without the actual bacon! This dog-safe version works perfectly in a treat ball, but also makes a great addition sprinkled through frozen Kong fillers, doggy ice cream, or on top of your pup's dinner as a garnish. It's an easy, handy, and versatile little snack.

1 tablespoon apple cider vinegar
1 tablespoon pure maple syrup
1½ teaspoons turmeric
2 cups raw coconut flakes

1. Preheat oven to 150°C / 300°F. Line a flat baking tray with baking paper.

2. Whisk apple cider vinegar, maple syrup, and turmeric in a small bowl.

3. Place raw coconut flakes in a bowl and pour the liquid mixture over the flakes. Gently stir through the mixture thoroughly until fully coated.

4. Spread your mixture thinly across your lined baking tray.

5. Bake for 12–15 minutes, turning the mixture around every 4 minutes to avoid burning. The coconut will turn golden when ready.

6. Remove from oven and allow to cool. The Coconut Bacon will harden and go crisp when fully cooled.

TURMERIC: *A powerful anti-inflammatory, turmeric helps promote general wellbeing and joint wellness. For dogs with ongoing disease or health issues, turmeric may not be advisable—always check with your vet before feeding.*

CHICKPEA CRUNCH

———— FILLS APPROXIMATELY 3 KONGS, OR CAN BE SERVED INDIVIDUALLY. ————

While this recipe may seem plain to the naked eye, there's something about the pack of protein in a satisfying crunch that makes dogs go gaga. Pop them into your dog's treat ball and watch them work for their snack. And, you may be sneaking some for yourself!

1 can chickpeas
1 tablespoon coconut oil, melted
2 teaspoons fresh thyme

HANDY HINT: *A rich source of protein and fiber, chickpeas also are packed with potassium, magnesium, and folate— all essentials for optimum pupper health. While plain chickpeas make a great doggie snack, hummus spreads or chickpea blends with onion and garlic are toxic to dogs and should be avoided.*

1. Preheat oven to 135°C / 275°F. Line a flat baking tray with baking paper.

2. Drain and empty chickpeas into a large bowl, and add melted coconut oil and thyme.

3. Massage the mixture thoroughly until chickpeas are fully coated.

4. Spread your mixture thinly across your lined baking tray.

5. Bake for 45 minutes, or until crunchy. Remove from oven and allow to cool. Serve.

THYME: *Packed with vitamins C, A, and K, iron, manganese, calcium, and antioxidants, this little herb is a great immune system booster. Thyme has antiseptic, anti-spasmodic, and anti-bacterial properties, making it great for your dog's skin, brain function, and gastrointestinal health.*

APPLE CRUMBLE

—————————— MAKES APPROXIMATELY 20 TREAT CUBES. ——————————

This flavor is a great "starter recipe" for Kong stuffers. With minimal ingredients and simple steps, you can pour and freeze it directly into your Kong—or freeze it into cubes to stuff into your Kong at a later date. I like to add a few fresh berries for variation sometimes too!

6 apples (any variety will do)
½ teaspoon cinnamon
½ cup rolled oats

Ice cube trays required.

> **HANDY HINT:** *Smear a bit of peanut butter over the small hole at the base of the Kong to prevent any leakage when freezing.*

1. Quarter apples then cut into slices, ensuring all seeds and core are removed. Sprinkle with cinnamon.

2. Place apple slices in a saucepan and add just enough water to cover. Bring to boil, cover, then lower heat and simmer for 5 minutes or until softened.

3. Drain fruit from liquid and allow to cool, then puree in blender until smooth.

4. Add the rolled oats and stir through gently.

5. Pour mixture into ice cube trays/molds and freeze for a minimum of 4 hours or until frozen through.

6. When frozen, remove from ice cube trays and store in labeled Ziploc bags in freezer.

A LOVELY PAIR

———— MAKES APPROXIMATELY 20 TREAT CUBES. ————

Inspiration for this recipe actually came from cooking baby purees for my daughter. When I realized how much our dog enjoyed the mixture, I knew it would make a tasty Kong stuffer—and a healthy one to boot! The pears offset the bitterness of the cauliflower and make for an irresistible doggo treat.

6 pears
1 small cauliflower

Ice cube trays required.

HANDY HINT: *When cooking, if you can crush the pear slice with the back of a wooden spoon, it is tender enough to be pureed.*

1. Core and quarter pears, ensuring all core and pith are removed. Roughly slice cauliflower florets into small pieces.

2. Place pear and cauliflower in a steamer over boiling water. Cover and steam for 10 minutes or until softened.

3. Allow to cool, then add pears, cauliflower, and around ¼ cup of water to a blender and puree until smooth. Add in small amounts of water as required to achieve your desired consistency.

4. Pour mixture into ice cube trays and freeze for a minimum of 4 hours or until frozen through.

5. When frozen, remove from ice cube trays and store in labeled Ziploc bags in freezer.

CAULIFLOWER: *Low in calories, but high in fiber, folate, and Vitamin K, cauliflower is a healthy snack that helps digestion and inflammation in dogs. It also make a great treat for dogs on calorie restrictions.*

CHUNKY DOGGIE

——————— MAKES APPROXIMATELY 20 TREAT CUBES. ———————

A play on the Ben & Jerry's classic "Chunky Monkey" ice cream, this recipe can be frozen directly into your Kong, or it can be added to an ice cream maker to turn into actual doggie ice cream. Either way, it'll be a hit for your pupper!

2 small bananas
2 cups plain organic yogurt
1 tablespoon honey
½ cup natural carob drops

Ice cube trays required.

1. Peel and chop bananas into small pieces.

2. Combine yogurt, banana, and honey in a blender and puree until smooth.

3. Add the carob drops and stir through gently.

4. Pour the puree mixture into ice cube trays and freeze for a minimum of 4 hours or until frozen through.

5. When frozen, remove from ice cube trays and store in labeled Ziploc bags in freezer.

BANANAS: *An excellent source of potassium, vitamins B-6, and C, bananas are as beneficial as they are tasty!*

VERY BERRY BITES

MAKES APPROXIMATELY 20 TREAT CUBES.

Blueberries make a fab addition to your pup's diet and this blend is a refreshing mix for the summer. Dogs love the surprise of whole blueberries to chomp on as the mixture melts.

---

2 cups plain organic yogurt
½ cup fresh blueberries

Ice cube trays required.

> **HANDY HINT:** *To make a yummy summer popsicle treat for yourself instead, add 2 tablespoons honey and a dash of lemon juice to the recipe!*

1. Wash blueberries under cold running water. Remove stems, leaves, and any crushed fruit.

2. Combine 1 cup yogurt and approximately half of your berries in blender and puree until smooth.

3. Pour the puree mixture into ice cube trays, alternating between the puree mix, spoonfuls of the plain yogurt, and whole blueberries to provide variation.

4. Freeze for a minimum of 4 hours or until frozen through.

5. When frozen, remove from ice cube trays and store in labeled Ziploc bags in freezer.

BLUEBERRIES: *High in vitamin C and fiber, blueberries are packed with antioxidants known to boost cognitive functions in dogs.*

KIWI CRUSH

––––––––––– MAKES APPROXIMATELY 20 TREAT CUBES. –––––––––––

The tart taste of this filling makes it a popular choice for warmer months, while the crunch of the cucumber is a pleasant textural surprise for your pup. If your pooch isn't a fan of the chunky cucumber, simply add the cucumber slices to the blender with the kiwi and pears to make a 100% smooth treat.

4 kiwis
4 pears
1 cucumber

Ice cube trays required.

1. Peel kiwi, and roughly slice into small pieces. Core and quarter pears, ensuring all core and pith are removed. Finely dice cucumber into small pieces, making sure to cut off and discard the ends.

2. Scatter all diced cucumber pieces and a few of the kiwi pieces into the base of your ice cube trays.

3. Add sliced pears and the remaining kiwi to blender. Puree until smooth. Add in small amounts of water as required to achieve your desired consistency.

4. Pour puree mixture into ice cube trays on top of the cucumber/kiwi and freeze for a minimum of 4 hours or until frozen through.

5. When frozen, remove from ice cube trays and store in labeled Ziploc bags in freezer.

KIWI: *High in potassium, fiber, and Vitamin C, kiwis are also a great source of select phytonutrients that are believed to help protect against age-related macular degeneration (vision loss) in dogs.*

PINK LADY

MAKES APPROXIMATELY 20 TREAT CUBES.

These perfectly pink frozen treats are bursting with the strong flavors of pink lady apples and cranberries—not to mention all the vitamins and minerals they have. With a tart initial taste followed by a sweet finish, they're sure to be a hit with your favorite pooch.

6 Pink Lady apples
1 handful fresh cranberries

Ice cube trays required.

> **HANDY HINT:** *For a fresh and fun twist on this recipe, add a small layer of coconut milk or yogurt in the base of your ice cube tray before pouring in your puree.*

1. Peel, core, and slice apples, ensuring all seeds and stems are removed.

2. Place apple slices and cranberries in a saucepan and cover with water. Bring to boil, cover, then lower heat and simmer for 5–10 minutes or until softened.

3. Drain liquid from fruit, setting the liquid aside. Allow to cool, then puree in blender until smooth. Add in small amounts of cooking liquid as required to achieve your desired consistency.

4. Pour mixture into ice cube trays and freeze for a minimum of 4 hours or until frozen through.

5. When frozen, remove from ice cube trays and store in labeled Ziploc bags in freezer.

I CARRIED A WATERMELON

—————————— **MAKES APPROXIMATELY 20 TREAT CUBES.** ——————————

This fruity blend is a hit in summer. I sometimes keep a few small chunks of fruit whole and add them into the Kong with the puree, for an added element of surprise. Remember to ensure the watermelon is seedless, as ingesting watermelon seeds can be harmful to dogs.

¼ fresh seedless watermelon
4 kiwi, peeled

Ice cube trays required.

> **HANDY HINT:** *For distinct linear layers between different ingredients, pop your ice cube trays in the freezer for an hour or so after you add each layer. Then once the first layer is frozen, go back, add your next layer, and continue until done!*

1. Slice the watermelon into cubes, ensuring all rind has been removed.

2. Roughly slice kiwi into small pieces.

3. Puree the watermelon pieces in blender and blend until smooth. Fill each ice cube tray halfway with the watermelon puree.

4. Puree the kiwi pieces in blender and blend until smooth. Pour the kiwi puree into the ice cube trays on top of the watermelon and freeze for a minimum of 4 hours or until frozen through.

5. When frozen, remove from ice cube trays and store in labeled Ziploc bags in freezer.

WATERMELON: *Just like the name suggests, watermelons are packed with water, making them an ideal option for rehydrating your pup in hot weather.*

MUTT MOJITO

—————— MAKES APPROXIMATELY 20 TREAT CUBES. ——————

A healthy and fresh flavor combination, this treat works double duty—great as a refresher in summer, but also tastes great warmed up and added to your dog's meal in cooler months. Packed with nourishing greens, it's a year-round winner.

4 zucchini
A few leaves of fresh mint
2 cups peas (fresh or frozen)

Ice cube trays required.

1. Roughly chop zucchini into small pieces, making sure to cut off and discard the ends. Finely chop mint leaves.

2. Place zucchini and peas in a steamer over boiling water. Cover and steam for 10–15 minutes or until softened.

3. Allow to cool, then add zucchini, peas, mint, and around ¼ cup of water to blender and puree until smooth. Add in small amounts of water as required to achieve your desired consistency.

4. Pour mixture into ice cube trays and freeze for a minimum of 4 hours or until frozen through.

5. When frozen, remove from ice cube trays and store in labeled Ziploc bags in freezer.

ZUCCHINI: *Packed full of vitamins, zucchinis are a top choice for dogs watching their waistline. These little beauties fill up your pup with barely any extra calories.*

TROPICAL PUNCH PUREE

──────── MAKES APPROXIMATELY 20 TREAT CUBES. ────────

I'm going to be honest and say this puree, while it makes an excellent Kong filler, also makes a fantastic popsicle that you can share with your doggo. You can even add a dash of sugar to yours for a hint of sweetness.

1 mango
½ pineapple
1 cup coconut milk (100% organic)

Ice cube trays required.

HANDY HINT: *For the best health and safety benefits, always opt for fresh fruits over canned or packaged varieties.*

1. Slice the mango into cubes, making sure to remove all the skin and stone. Ensure the pit is discarded entirely, to avoid being swallowed and stuck in a dog's digestive tract.

2. Wash pineapple under cold running water. Roughly slice the pineapple into small pieces, making sure to cut off and discard the central core, spiky skin, and ends.

3. Combine coconut milk, mango, and pineapple pieces in blender and blend until smooth.

4. Pour mixture into ice cube trays and freeze for a minimum of 4 hours or until frozen through.

5. When frozen, remove from ice cube trays and store in labeled Ziploc bags in freezer.

PINEAPPLE: *This tropical delight is packed with a bunch of vitamins and minerals, making it a healthy addition to your pupper's diet. It is, however, high in sugar, so should be limited to treats in small quantities only.*

HEARTY BUTTERNUT SQUASH SOUP

——— MAKES APPROXIMATELY 20 TREAT CUBES. ———

Classic butternut squash and ginger unite in this traditional soup. Serve frozen in the summer or heat up and add to your dog's dinner for a timeless winter dish.

1 butternut squash
½ tablespoon freshly ground ginger
1 tablespoon organic coconut oil (melted)

Ice cube trays required.

BUTTERNUT SQUASH/ PUMPKIN: *A great choice for pooches with sensitive stomachs, these are a top source of fiber, promoting healthy digestion.*

1. Preheat oven to 200°C / 400°F.

2. Peel and roughly slice squash into small pieces, making sure to cut off and discard the ends and seeds.

3. Add squash, ginger, and coconut oil to an oven tray and toss gently until all pieces are coated.

4. Bake for approximately 20 minutes or until softened, then remove from oven and allow to cool.

5. Add squash pieces to blender with ¼ cup water and puree until smooth. Add in more water as required to achieve your desired consistency.

6. Pour mixture into ice cube trays and freeze for a minimum of 4 hours or until frozen through.

7. When frozen, remove from ice cube trays and store in labeled Ziploc bags in freezer.

Biscuits & Snacks

Dog biscuits and snacks are one of the easiest, no-fuss ways to treat your dog.

In an airtight container, a batch of biscuits can last you the full week, without worrying about any treats melting, or frosting going bad.

These recipes are a great alternative to store-bought bones or biscuits, and because you made them, you know exactly what's in them—no hidden nasties, preservatives, or recalls to worry about.

While other treats may make a better training treat or Kong stuffer, these biscuits and snacks are handy everyday treats your dog is sure to love.

HANDY HINT: *The amount of coconut flour you add to the mixture depends on your brand of flour and size of your eggs. If your dough is still too wet after adding 3 tablespoons of coconut flour, simply add one tablespoon more at a time until you reach a doughy, non-sticky consistency.*

"CHOC"-CHIP COOKIES

——————— MAKES 12 "CHOC"-CHIP COOKIES. ———————

Is there anything more irresistible than a choc-chip cookie straight from the oven? This dog-friendly version uses pet-safe carob chips that are as healthy as they are tasty!

1½ cups almond flour
1 tablespoon coconut oil
2 eggs, beaten
3 tablespoons coconut flour
½ cup natural carob drops

1. Preheat oven to 165°C / 325°F. Line a large cookie sheet with baking paper.

2. With an electric mixer, mix almond flour and coconut oil on low speed until combined.

3. Add the eggs to the mixture and mix on medium speed for 2 minutes.

4. Add in one tablespoon of coconut flour at a time and mix on medium speed, scraping down the sides of the bowl between each teaspoon of coconut flour. Your mixture will form a dough.

5. Add the carob drops and stir through gently until incorporated throughout.

6. Scoop out bite-sized pieces with a spoon, roll into little balls, and place on lined tray. Flatten each cookie with the back of a spoon. (The cookies will not spread during baking.)

7. Place your cookies onto your cookie sheet and bake for 15 minutes or until golden.

CAROB: *The healthy alternative to the doggie no-no, chocolate, carob is packed with vitamins B1, A, and iron, making it a popular sweet treat. Opt for gluten- and dairy-free varieties.*

HANDY HINT: *No cookie cutter? Just cut your dough into squares. Your dog won't mind—we promise!*

CAMPFIRE S'MORES

———————— MAKES 10–12 CAMPFIRE S'MORES CRACKERS. ————————

As an Australian, I grew up having a huge fascination with American snacks—and s'mores topped that list (I blame my obsession with The Babysitters Club). While marshmallows and chocolate may be out, this recipe still hits that gooey sweet spot.

Crackers:
1 cup almond flour
1 egg
¼ cup low-sodium
   vegetable stock
5 tablespoons
   coconut flour

Filling:
¼ cup natural carob
   drops
4 oz. cream cheese

Cracker Instructions:

1. Preheat oven to 175°C / 345°F. Line a large cookie sheet with baking paper.

2. With an electric mixer, combine almond flour, egg, and vegetable stock on low speed until combined, then mix on medium speed for another 2 minutes.

3. Add in 1–2 tablespoons of coconut flour at a time and mix on medium speed, scraping down the sides of the bowl between each addition of coconut flour. Your mixture will form a dough.

4. Roll your dough into a ball and place on a sheet of baking paper. Slightly flatten the dough and place another sheet of baking paper on top. Then roll your dough to around ¼-inch thickness.

5. Place your rolled dough on a cutting board and leave in the fridge for 20

minutes. This chills the dough, making it less sticky and easier to cut designs that hold their shape.

6. Remove your dough from fridge and, using a medium-sized bone-shaped cookie cutter, cut out the biscuits and place on a lined cookie sheet. Repeat until dough is finished (you don't need to re-refrigerate the dough).

7. *Optional:* Using alphabet cookie stamps, stamp your dog's name or a special message into your s'mores crackers.

8. Bake crackers for 10–15 minutes or until golden and crunchy. Place on a baking rack to cool, then fill and serve.

Filling Instructions:

1. Place carob drops in a heat safe bowl. Melt the drops over boiling water, stirring constantly as they melt to a thick consistency.

2. Spread a dollop of the melted carob chips onto your crackers with a smear of cream cheese and top with another cracker.

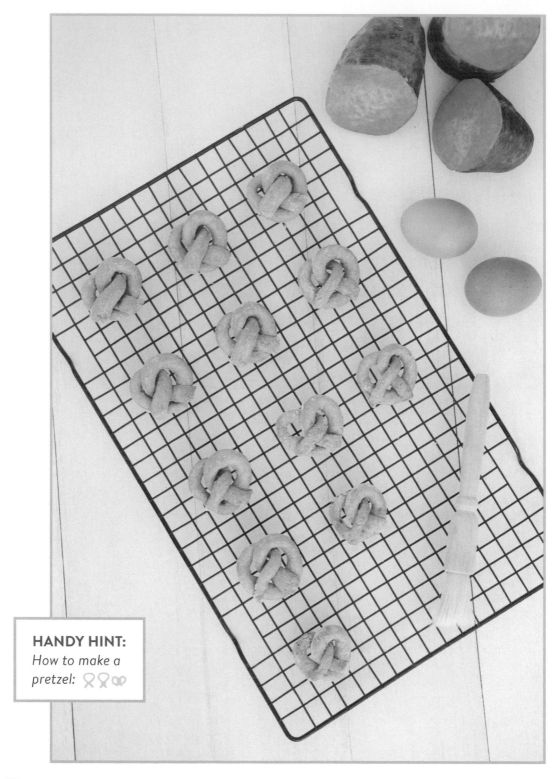

HANDY HINT:
How to make a pretzel: 👋👋👐

SWEET POTATO PRETZELS

——————— **MAKES APPROXIMATELY 20 PRETZELS.** ———————

These pretzels are making me thirsty! I have to say, this recipe is one of my most popular recipes to date. It's healthy, not too complicated, and makes such a cool snack in a world of boring dog biscuits.

1 large sweet potato
1¾ cups whole wheat flour
1 tablespoon flaxseed meal
1 egg

1. Preheat oven to 175°C / 345°F. Line a flat cookie sheet with baking paper.

2. Peel and dice sweet potato into cubes, and place in a saucepan, adding just enough water to cover. Bring to boil, cover, then lower heat and simmer for 10 minutes or until softened.

3. Drain sweet potato and allow to cool. Puree in blender or food processor.

4. Combine flour and flaxseed in a large bowl.

5. Beat egg and set aside a small amount (approx. 1 tablespoon) to use as an egg wash later.

6. Add sweet potato puree and remaining beaten egg to dry ingredients. Mix with a wooden spoon until the mixture forms a dough.

7. Take a bite-sized piece of dough and roll into a 10-inch tube (about the thickness of a pencil).

8. Take each tube and make it into a U shape, twist the ends together, and fold back to form the pretzel shape. Ensure the ends of the pretzel are tucked under and secured.

9. Place the pretzels onto the lined cookie sheet. Using a pastry brush, brush the remaining beaten egg lightly on top of the pretzels. Place in the oven.

10. Bake for 25 minutes or until golden brown. Cool and serve.

PEANUT BUTTER POPCORN

———— MAKES 1 SERVING OF POPCORN FOR YOU AND YOUR DOG TO SHARE. ————

Full disclosure: I often find myself snacking throughout the process of making this treat. I mean, popcorn, PB, and maple syrup? What's not to love? And the microwave popcorn hack below gives me life.

2 tablespoons popcorn kernels (makes approx. 3–4 cups cooked popcorn)
⅓ cup organic peanut butter
1 tablespoon pure maple syrup

HANDY HINT: *Air popped popcorn is ideal, as it uses no vegetable oils for cooking. If you don't have an air popper, simply pour plain kernels into a brown paper lunch bag, fold over the top of the bag twice firmly to seal it closed, and microwave for 1½ minutes, or until the popping slows.*

1. Preheat oven to 160°C / 320°F. Line a flat baking tray with baking paper.

2. Pop kernels in your favorite air popper. (Don't have an air popper? See our Handy Hint.) Once cooked, place your popcorn in a large bowl. Ensure all kernels are popped fully and any uncooked kernels are removed.

3. Drizzle the peanut butter and maple syrup evenly over your cooked popcorn and stir through until fully coated.

4. Spread your coated popcorn on the lined baking tray and cook for 5–7 minutes or until golden brown. Cool slightly and serve warm.

POPCORN: *Popcorn contains the healthy trio of potassium, magnesium, and calcium that supports bone health and immune system strength.*

HANDY HINT: *If you ever find a dog treat cookie dough is too sticky, add a tablespoon or two of coconut flour to dry it out. Coconut flour is extraordinarily absorbent and can often help bring a wet dough back to life.*

FRESH BREATH DOG TREATS

———————————— MAKES APPROXIMATELY 12 FRESH BREATH DOG TREATS. ————————————

Who doesn't want a dog with fresher breath? These yummy bone biscuits are a great staple treat to have around—especially when your pup may be a bit on the stinky side!

1 cup rice flour
1 tablespoon coconut oil
1 tablespoon honey
2 eggs
3 tablespoons coconut flour
¼ cup fresh mint, finely chopped

1. Preheat oven to 175°C / 345°F. Line a flat cookie sheet with baking paper.
2. With an electric mixer, mix rice flour, coconut oil, and honey on low speed until combined.
3. Add eggs to the mixture and mix on medium speed for 2 minutes.
4. Add in one tablespoon of coconut flour at a time and mix on medium speed, scraping down the sides of the bowl between each tablespoon of coconut flour. Your mixture will form a dough.
5. Add finely chopped mint and stir through gently until incorporated throughout. Roll your dough into a ball and place on a sheet of baking paper. Slightly flatten the dough and place another sheet of baking paper on top. Then roll your dough to around ¼-inch thickness.
6. Place your rolled dough on a cutting board and leave in the fridge for 20 minutes. This chills the dough, making it less sticky and easier to cut designs that hold their shape.
7. Remove your dough from fridge and, using a medium-sized bone-shaped cookie cutter, cut out the biscuits and place on lined cookie sheet. Repeat until dough is finished (you don't need to re-refrigerate the dough).
8. Bake cookies for 10–15 minutes or until golden and crunchy. Place on a baking rack to cool, then serve.

MINT: *Fresh mint is a great way to keep your dog's breath smelling sweet, and also has the added effect of calming an upset stomach.*

QUINOA & FLAXSEED RECHARGE BISCUITS

—————— MAKES APPROXIMATELY 15–20 RECHARGE BISCUITS. ——————

I love these little biscuits. They require minimal effort, no rolling or cutting, and are packed full of nourishing superfoods. Dogs love the crunchy texture too.

¾ cup rice flour
¼ cup flaxseed meal
3 tablespoons coconut oil
1 egg
1 banana, mashed
3 tablespoons quinoa flour

1. Preheat oven to 175°C / 345°F. Line a flat cookie sheet with baking paper.

2. With an electric mixer, mix rice flour, flaxseed meal, coconut oil, and egg on low speed until combined.

3. Add the mashed banana to the mixture and mix on low speed until just combined.

4. Add the quinoa flour one tablespoon at a time, being sure to scrape down the sides of the bowl each time. Your mixture will form a crumbly dough.

5. Scoop out bite-sized pieces with a spoon and roll into little balls. Place on a flat cookie sheet with baking paper. Gently flatten each ball with the back of a fork to make a cookie shape.

6. Bake for 10 minutes, then flip your biscuits and bake for another 5 minutes. Place on a baking rack to cool, then serve.

FLAXSEED MEAL: *The omega-3 fatty acids found in flaxseed meal promote healthy skin and glossy coats in dogs.*

PUMPKIN & CHIA BISCUITS

——— MAKES APPROXIMATELY 20 BISCUITS. ———

These yummy little biscuits are a great addition to any doggie cookie jar. If you're looking for a variation, try replacing the plain pumpkin puree with our Hearty Butternut Squash Soup puree—just skip adding the ¼ cup water in that recipe (page 63).

7 oz. fresh pumpkin, peeled and diced
1 cup whole wheat flour
1 egg, beaten
4–6 tablespoons coconut flour
1 teaspoon black chia seeds

1. Preheat oven to 175°C / 345°F. Line a flat cookie sheet with baking paper.

2. Place pumpkin cubes in a saucepan, adding just enough water to cover. Bring to boil, cover, then lower heat and simmer for 10 minutes or until softened.

3. Drain pumpkin and allow to cool. Puree in blender or food processor. Transfer to a mixing bowl.

4. Combine flour, pumpkin, and egg with a mixer on low speed.

5. Once combined, add in one tablespoon of coconut flour at a time and mix on medium speed, scraping down the sides between each addition. (Depending on your pumpkin puree and egg size, you may not need all of the coconut flour).

6. Roll your dough into a ball and place on a sheet of baking paper. Slightly flatten and place another sheet of baking paper on top. Then roll your dough to around ¼–½-inch thickness.

7. Place rolled dough on a cutting board and refrigerate for 20 minutes. This makes the dough less sticky and easier to cut designs that hold their shape.

8. Use a medium-sized bone-shaped cookie cutter to cut out the biscuits and place on lined cookie sheet. Repeat until dough is finished (you don't need to re-refrigerate).

9. Sprinkle biscuits lightly with chia seeds and bake for 15–20 minutes or until golden and crunchy. Cool and serve.

> **CHIA:** *With seven times more Vitamin C than oranges, eight times more omega-3 than salmon, and six times more fiber than oat bran, chia is a powerful addition to your dog's diet.*

HANDY HINT: *Golden syrup can be interchanged with molasses in this recipe.*

ANZAC DOG BISCUITS

—————— MAKES 16 ANZAC BISCUITS. ——————

ANZAC Biscuits are a hundred-year-old tradition in Australia. This easy to make sweet treat was sent from homes to Australian and New Zealand soldiers (ANZACS) serving in World War I. A chewy treat, this recipe uses all dog-friendly ingredients.

1¼ cups whole wheat flour
1 cup rolled oats
¾ cups desiccated coconut (if you cannot find this, use unsweetened shredded coconut)
1 cup natural applesauce
3 tablespoons golden syrup

1. Preheat oven to 175°C / 345°F. Line a flat cookie sheet with baking paper.

2. Combine flour, oats, and coconut in a bowl.

3. Mix the applesauce and golden syrup in a separate bowl, then add to the dry ingredients. Mix together until fully combined.

4. Scoop out bite-sized pieces with a spoon and roll into little balls, and place on lined cookie sheet. Flatten each cookie with the back of a fork.

5. Bake cookies for 12–15 minutes or until golden brown. Place on baking rack to cool and serve.

ROLLED OATS: *An excellent source of dietary fiber and iron, rolled oats in small quantities can assist in healthy digestion and increased energy levels for lethargic dogs.*

DOGGO GINGER SNAPS

───────── MAKES 20–30 GINGER SNAPS. ─────────

These crunchy little snaps are such a versatile dog treat. Sure, you can serve them as suggested in cookie form, but you can also crunch them up and sprinkle them as extra layers in Kongs or break them into small pieces and hide them in treat balls. And did I mention they are delicious?

2 cups almond flour
½ cup coconut flour
½ cup organic peanut butter
3 tablespoons ground ginger
1 tablespoon cinnamon
¼ cup water

> **HANDY HINT:** *These sugar-free snacks make an excellent treat during the holiday season and go perfectly with our Doggie Royal Icing (page 156).*

1. Preheat oven to 165°C / 325°F. Line a flat cookie sheet with baking paper.

2. Mix all ingredients together in a large bowl and form a ball of dough.

3. Split your dough into two sections. For each section, roll your dough into a ball and place on a sheet of baking paper. Slightly flatten the dough and place another sheet of baking paper on top. Then roll your dough to around ¼-inch thickness.

4. Repeat for the second section of dough then place both sections of rolled dough on a cutting board and leave in the fridge for 20 minutes. This chills the dough, making it less sticky and easier to cut designs that hold their shape.

5. Remove your dough from fridge and, using a round cookie cutter, cut out the biscuits and place on the lined cookie sheet. Repeat until dough is finished (you don't need to re-refrigerate the dough).

6. Bake for 25 minutes, then turn off the oven and leave them in the oven for 45 further minutes, or until crisp.

2-INGREDIENT PUP SNACKS

────────────── MAKES 20–30 PUP SNACKS. ──────────────

Can we just get a holla for easy dog treat recipes? A lot of 2-ingredient recipes call for processed ingredients, but these snacks are as healthy as they are simple.

½ cup organic black beans
   (soaked overnight, drained,
   and cooked)
½ cup almond flour

1. Preheat oven to 175°C / 345°F. Line a flat cookie sheet with baking paper.

2. Using a fork, mash the drained black beans in a bowl.

3. When they are mostly mashed, add in almond flour little by little, mixing in between.

4. Roll dough onto floured surface to approximately ¼-inch thickness.

5. Using your favorite cookie cutter, cut out the biscuits and place on the lined cookie sheet. Repeat steps 4 and 5 until the dough is finished.

6. Bake for 15 minutes, flip, and bake for another 15 minutes. If still soft, turn the temperature down to 90°C / 195°F and let set until crunchy.

BLACK BEANS: *These little beans pack a powerful punch of protein and fiber. Always feed them in moderation to avoid gas and constipation in your dog. I've recommended cooking them yourself as many canned beans contain high levels of sodium.*

Cakes & Slices

Perfect for parties, special occasions, and pupper get-togethers, these cakes and slices are great to share among friends.

Because they take a bit more effort and time than easier recipes (like our No-Bake Dog Treats and Kong & Treat Ball Stuffers), I tend to make them when I know they're going to be enjoyed by a larger group.

The biggest thing to get used to when baking dog-friendly cakes and slices is that the ingredients are all so different from your normal cakes filled with butter and sugar. This means your methods of baking are varied and it does take some practice to learn how to frost cakes with doggie icing, or know when to turn a pup-friendly pancake!

But believe me, when you serve these beauties up to dog loving friends, it'll make it all worthwhile.

HANDY HINT: *Have a smaller-sized pooch? Try mini muffin tins for bite-sized pupcakes.*

CARROT PUPCAKES

Don't be deceived by the look of these pupcakes. Packed with nutritious ingredients, they actually provide quite the crunchy snack for your furry friend.

1 cup grated carrot
2 eggs, beaten
¼ cup applesauce
1½ cups whole wheat flour
¼ cup rolled oats
2 teaspoons cinnamon

1. Preheat oven to 175°C / 345°F. Lightly grease 6 cupcake molds.

2. Combine grated carrot, beaten eggs, and applesauce in a medium bowl.

3. Combine flour, oats, and cinnamon in a large bowl.

4. Slowly add the wet ingredients to the dry ingredients to form a thick, heavy batter.

5. Spoon the mixture evenly into the cupcake tin ensuring they are filled, as the mixture will not rise.

6. Bake in the oven for 20 minutes.

7. Remove from oven, allow to cool in pan for 5 minutes, and then transfer to cooling racks.

8. When completely cooled, ice your pupcakes with our Pup-Friendly Cream Cheese Frosting (page 154)

CARROT: *In addition to containing lots of vitamins that help maintain good eye health and vision, carrots are a high density, low calorie food option, making them the perfect addition for weight loss and management in dogs.*

HANDY HINT: *Does your pup prefer their Oat Bars chewy rather than crunchy? Simply remove them from the oven 5 minutes earlier!*

APPLE PIE OAT BARS

— MAKES 12 MEDIUM BARS. —

Let's go apple picking! These spiced apple bars make great snacks to share, and can also be used as a tasty crumbled layer when stuffing Kongs. Gotta love a versatile treat.

2 small apples
3 cups rolled oats
2 teaspoons cinnamon
¼ cup applesauce
¼ cup honey
1–2 tablespoons warm water

1. Preheat oven to 180°C / 350°F. Line an 11 x 7 x 2" pan with baking paper.

2. Peel and core both apples, ensuring all seeds are removed. Finely dice apple in small cubes (approximately ¼ x ¼ inch).

3. Combine diced apple, oats, and cinnamon in a large bowl.

4. Combine applesauce, honey, and water.

5. Add the wet ingredients to the dry ingredients and mix until combined.

6. Firmly press the mixture into lined baking pan.

7. Bake for 40 minutes or until crisp.

8. Remove from oven and allow to cool completely in pan.

9. Slice into bite-sized bars and serve.

APPLES: *As well as being a good source of dietary fiber and vitamin C, apples contain omega-3 fatty acids that have been known to help to control skin allergies.*

PUP-FRIENDLY BANANA BREAD

—————— MAKES ONE BANANA BREAD LOAF. ——————

One of the things I love about this recipe is it's totally human friendly. It may not have the sugar kick of regular banana bread, but it's just as delicious! So grab a slice for you and a slice for your doggo.

2 tablespoons coconut
    oil, melted
3 eggs
1 cup almond flour
½ cup coconut flour
½ teaspoon baking soda
1 teaspoon cinnamon
3 overripe bananas,
    mashed
1 tablespoon honey

1. Preheat oven to 180°C / 350°F. Lightly grease and line an 8 x 4" pan.
2. Mix the coconut oil and eggs in a large bowl until well combined.
3. Combine almond flour, coconut flour, baking soda, and cinnamon in a separate bowl. Mix together and make a well in the center.
4. Add the oil and egg mixture and stir until well combined.
5. Add the mashed bananas and honey, and gently stir through until just combined.
6. Spoon the mixture into the prepared pan and smooth the top.
7. Bake for 25–30 minutes or until golden brown and a skewer comes out clean.
8. Remove from oven, allow to cool in pan for 5 minutes, and then transfer to cooling racks.

HONEY: *Packed with energy, a small amount of honey has been known to help with allergies and lethargy in dogs.*

PUPPY PANCAKES

—————————— MAKES 8–10 SMALL PUPPY PANCAKES. ——————————

This simple recipe is a staple favorite in our house, and the use of rice flour makes for a lighter mixture than other denser dog-friendly pancake variations.

2 eggs
1 cup plain organic yogurt
1 tablespoon honey
½ cup rice flour
½ teaspoon cinnamon

> **HANDY HINT:** *Batter too thick? Add a teaspoon or two of warm water to thin out the mixture. Batter too runny? Add a tablespoon of rice flour and whisk through to get the right consistency.*

1. In a medium bowl, whisk together the eggs, yogurt, and honey.

2. Whisk in the rice flour and cinnamon. You will be left with a smooth pancake batter.

3. Heat a greased pan to a low heat and spoon the batter to form a small pancake.

4. Wait about 1–2 minutes until the first side cooks before flipping the pancake and cooking the other side.

5. Serve plain, with a sprinkle of cinnamon or fresh berries.

HANDY HINT: *Get creative with your doggie donut toppings! Try raspberries, liver sprinkles, or drizzled carob for variation.*

DOGGO DONUTS

Of all my recipes, this is the number one recipe I get the most feedback about and have seen the most imitations of. I think it comes down to the fact that, human or doggo, we all love our donuts!

Donuts:
1 cup whole wheat flour
1 teaspoon cinnamon
½ cup applesauce
2 tablespoons honey
1 egg, beaten
3 tablespoons warm water

Icing:
¼ cup plain yogurt drops

1. Preheat oven to 175°C / 345°F. Lightly grease 6 wells of a regular donut tray.

2. Combine flour and cinnamon in large bowl.

3. Add applesauce, honey, and egg to a small bowl and whisk until well combined.

4. Add the wet ingredients to the dry ingredients and mix to form a thick batter.

5. Mix in the warm water if the batter is too dry.

6. Fill each donut mold to the top.

7. Bake for 20 minutes or until cooked through. To test, insert a toothpick into the donut. If it comes out clean, the donuts are ready and can be removed from the oven.

8. Allow to cool completely, then remove from pan.

9. Melt the yogurt drops in a small heat-safe bowl over boiling water.

10. Dip each donut in the yogurt. Set aside on a baking rack to set, and serve.

HANDY HINT: *This makes a full tray, which is far too much for one dog and best shared with friends.*

RASPBERRY & COCONUT BARK

MAKES APPROXIMATELY 20 LARGE PIECES.

Bark if you love this twist on a sweet classic! Once you've mastered the basic recipe below I encourage you to get creative with your bark, adding other fresh berries and dog-friendly ingredients for your own personalized, pet-friendly bark.

2½ cups natural carob drops
2½ cups plain yogurt drops
1 cup fresh raspberries
½ cup desiccated coconut (if you cannot find this, use unsweetened shredded coconut)

1. Line an 11 x 7 x 2" pan with baking paper.

2. Melt the carob drops in a small heat-safe bowl over boiling water, stirring constantly.

3. Pour melted carob evenly into pan, ensuring the bottom surface is fully covered. Place in the refrigerator to set. Chill for approximately 30 minutes or until firm.

4. Melt the yogurt drops in a small heat-safe bowl over boiling water, stirring constantly.

5. Pour half the melted yogurt into pan on top of the carob layer.

6. Scatter raspberries and coconut throughout pan mixture and pour remaining melted yogurt on top, spreading evenly.

7. Place in the refrigerator to set. Chill for approximately 45 minutes or until firm.

8. Break into pieces and serve.

RASPBERRIES: *Raspberries provide a good source of dietary fiber and have a low energy density, allowing your pup to enjoy a sweet treat while leaving them fuller for longer.*

"CHOCOLATE" CUPCAKES

——————— MAKES 12 "CHOCOLATE" CUPCAKES ———————

These cupcakes make the perfect addition to any doggie party—or just a regular Saturday at home! As with most dog cakes, the mixture is slightly heavier than a normal cake batter, making a denser doggo cake.

½ cup coconut oil
2 eggs
½ cup rice flour
2 tablespoons carob powder
½ teaspoon baking soda

> **HANDY HINT:** *When spooning the mixture into the mini cupcake pan, gently roll into small balls and press into the tin for a smooth cupcake shape.*

1. Preheat oven to 175°C / 345°F. Lightly grease a mini cupcake pan (12 mini cupcake molds).

2. With an electric mixer, mix coconut oil and eggs on medium speed until well combined.

3. Combine rice flour, carob powder, and baking soda in a separate bowl and give a quick stir to combine.

4. Add dry mixture to the wet, and mix together on medium speed for 3 minutes.

5. Gently spoon the mixture into the greased mini cupcake pan. You want your mixture to fill the cups halfway up with room to rise.

6. Bake for 12–15 minutes or until cupcakes spring back lightly when touched in the center.

7. Remove from oven, allow to cool in pan for 5 minutes, and then transfer to cooling racks.

8. When completely cooled, ice your cupcakes with our "Chocolate" Icing (page 156).

Chews

Dogs love chews. And dog owners do, too.

These longer lasting treats give dogs the chance to exercise their natural instinct of chewing and gnawing, and the ingredients couldn't be purer and simpler.

In this book, all of our recipes use a standard oven to dehydrate and bake chews. The treats in this chapter are basic chew recipes to get you started.

However, if you find your dog loves these recipes more than other treat varieties, I'd highly recommend investing in a food dehydrator.

Dehydrators allow you to batch-cook your treats in bulk without ever having to turn the oven on. As the dehydration process can take hours at a time, a dehydrator is often preferable for batch baking rather than an oven. There are many Facebook groups devoted to dehydrator dog treat cooking and it's a great way to get creative with making your own treats.

VEGGIE CHIPS

———— EACH VEGGIE MAKES APPROXIMATELY 12–20 CHIPS, DEPENDENT ON SIZE. ————

This biggest problem with this recipe is making sure you don't eat all the chips before your dog sees them! Get creative with your vegetable choices, ensuring they are all dog-safe varieties.

Light olive oil spray
Vegetable options (choose one or all!):
  1 medium beetroot
  1 small sweet potato
  2 carrots
  1 parsnip

> **HANDY HINT:** *Keep a watchful eye on your chips in the oven. Certain vegetable varieties will brown more quickly than others. Veggie Chips will be crispy and brown when ready, not burnt.*

1. Preheat oven to 190°C / 375°F. Line 2 flat baking trays with baking paper.

2. Wash your vegetables under cold running water.

3. Peel and slice all vegetables into paper thin slices. (A vegetable slicer or mandolin works best.)

4. Place your sliced veggies on paper towels and leave for 10 minutes to distribute moisture.

5. Place the veggie chips on lined baking tray, spray lightly with olive oil (less oil is better), and bake for 18–25 minutes.

6. Remove from oven, allow to cool on tray for 10 minutes, and then transfer to cooling racks. Serve.

SWEET POTATO: *Among the highest rated vegetables on the nutrition scale, sweet potatoes include vitamins A, C, manganese, and iron, which are good for a healthy coat and immune system.*

HANDY HINT: *Store your strips in an airtight container to keep them fresher for longer. If opting to marinate your strips, keep in mind the olive oil will shorten their shelf life.*

BBQ CHICKEN STRIPS

———————————— MAKES APPROXIMATELY 12 CHICKEN STRIPS. ————————————

This simple recipe is a firm favorite among the many doggo taste testers that have tried it. The chew of the chicken coupled with the rosemary flavor makes for a winning combination. This method uses a combination of dehydration and baking, making it much quicker than standard, fully dehydrated dog treats.

1 chicken breast, slightly thawed

Note: It is recommended to freeze meat for at least 1 week prior to turning it into chews. This helps kill any parasites in the meat.

Optional Marinade:
1 tablespoon olive oil
2 teaspoons fresh rosemary, stripped from
   stems and finely chopped

1. Preheat oven to 100°C / 210°F—select "Vent Bake" on your oven if you have that option. Line a flat baking tray with baking paper.

2. Slice the chicken breast into thin strips. (If your chicken is only slightly thawed it makes it easier to cut.)

3. If marinating your strips, toss them lightly through the olive oil and fresh rosemary until fully coated.

4. Place the chicken strips on lined baking tray, and bake for 3 hours. (If your oven doesn't have a "vent bake" option, after about 1½ hours you can open the oven door slightly and leave ajar to decrease moisture. Only do this if the environment is safe to do so. Do not leave your oven unattended.)

5. Increase the temperature to 150°C / 300°F and blast for 3 minutes at that temperature to kill any surface pathogens—this makes the treats safe for you to handle.

6. Remove from oven, allow to cool on tray for 10 minutes, and then transfer to cooling racks.

7. Cover with a tea towel and dry overnight at room temperature.

ROSEMARY: *Packed with iron and calcium, rosemary is also a natural antioxidant, making it a great herb to add to your dog's diet every now and then.*

BEEF JERKY

—————— MAKES APPROXIMATELY 20 PIECES OF BEEF JERKY. ——————

This is one of the easiest treats to make (just one ingredient!) but it does take an investment of your time. I suggest making it on a day when you're doing odd jobs at home and can check on the treats' progress every so often.

8 oz. lean ground beef

Note: It is recommended to freeze meat for at least 1 week prior to turning it into chews. This helps kill any parasites in the meat.

1. Preheat oven to 70°C / 160°F—select "Vent Bake" on your oven if you have that option. Line a flat baking tray with baking paper.

2. Place your ground beef on a sheet of baking paper. Slightly flatten and place another sheet of baking paper on top. Then, using a rolling pin, roll your ground beef flat to around ⅛-inch thickness.

3. Remove the top layer of baking paper. Using a knife, score the meat in a checkerboard pattern. These score lines will later be where your treats break apart into bite-sized pieces.

4. Keeping the scored, flattened ground beef on the piece of baking paper, slide it onto a baking tray and bake for 5 hours. (If your oven doesn't have a "vent bake" option, after about 1½ hours you can open the oven door slightly and leave ajar to decrease moisture. Only do this if the environment is safe to do so. Do not leave your oven unattended.)

5. Remove from oven, allow to cool on tray for 10 minutes, then break apart the treats at the score lines.

6. Place treats on a freshly lined baking tray and place back in the oven at 70°C / 160°F for another 2–3 hours or until fully dried. When your treats have finished cooking, increase the temperature to 150°C / 300°F and blast for 3 minutes at that temperature to kill any surface pathogens—this makes the treats safe for you to handle.

7. Remove from oven, allow to cool, and serve.

> **LEAN BEEF:** *Like their wild counterparts, dogs thrive on high-quality, lean animal protein. The option of lean beef provides the wealth of essential amino acids dogs need, but without the fat.*

CHICKEN & SWEET POTATO CHEWERS

---------- MAKES APPROXIMATELY 20 CHICKEN & SWEET POTATO CHEWERS. ----------

This recipe is practically a roast dinner in jerky form! This is another recipe that does take a considerable time investment though. If your dog favors these chewers, as well as the BBQ Chicken Strips (page 105) and Beef Jerky (page 106), I think you're definitively on track to look at investing in a dehydrator.

---

1 large sweet potato, peeled and diced
4 oz. ground chicken
1 teaspoon chia seeds

Note: It is recommended to freeze meat for at least 1 week prior to turning it into chews. This helps kill any parasites in the meat.

1. Preheat oven to 70°C / 160°F—select "Vent Bake" on your oven if you have that option. Line a flat baking tray with baking paper.

2. Place sweet potato cubes in a saucepan, adding just enough water to cover. Bring to boil, cover, then lower heat and simmer for 10 minutes or until softened.

> **HANDY HINT:** *Don't have a piping bag? A Ziploc bag with the end cut off works just as well!*

3. Drain sweet potato and while still warm, puree in food processor. Add in the chicken and chia; then puree until fully combined.

4. Place mixture into a piping bag and pipe out long lines onto your tray. The thicker the lines, the longer they will take to dehydrate in the oven. Bake for 10 hours until your treats are firm and not sticky. (If your oven doesn't have a "vent bake" option, after about 1½ hours you can open the oven door slightly and leave ajar to decrease moisture. Only do this if the environment is safe to do so. Do not leave your oven unattended.)

5. When your treats have finished cooking, increase the temperature to 150°C / 300°F and blast for 3 minutes to kill any surface pathogens—this makes the treats safe for you to handle.

6. Remove from oven, and allow to cool. While they are still warm to touch, cut in half or to your desired treat length.

HANDY HINT: *Your apple chews will crisp up when removed from the oven. To get the exact level of "crispiness" your dog prefers, test your chips during baking. When you think they're ready, remove one chip from the oven and leave out at room temperature for at least 5 minutes. If it's "crispy" to your exact preference, remove the rest of the chips from the oven. If not, you can leave them in for a bit longer.*

CRISPY APPLE CHEWS

—————— MAKES 20–25 APPLE CHEWS, DEPENDENT ON SIZE OF THE APPLES. ——————

The first time I tested this recipe I was expecting these chews not to be as popular as their meat-based alternatives. Boy, was I wrong! I don't know if it's the spice of the cinnamon, or the tang of the apple, but dogs can't get enough of these babies. And for the record, they're hands down one of the easiest treats to make.

2 apples (any variety will do)
¼ teaspoon cinnamon
¼ teaspoon ground ginger

1. Preheat oven to 80°C / 175°F. Line a flat baking tray with baking paper.

2. Wash and core both apples, ensuring all seeds are removed.

3. Slice apples into thin slices. Note: Paper thin slices will give a chip-like texture, and thicker ¼-inch slices will give a chewier treat.

4. Place the apple slices on lined baking tray, sprinkle with cinnamon and ginger, and bake for 2 hours, turning halfway through cooking.

5. Remove from oven, allow to cool on tray for 10 minutes, and then transfer to cooling racks. Serve once they are crispy.

CINNAMON: *Just a dash of this tasty spice can help regulate a dog's blood sugar and improves brain function. Studies have also shown its ability to assist dogs struggling with arthritis.*

BANANA CINNAMON CHIPS

———— MAKES 40 BANANA CINNAMON CHIPS, DEPENDENT ON THE SIZE OF BANANA. ————

These little chips are perfect stuffed in a Ziploc bag and taken on hikes and doggie outings. Their crunchy texture and yummy flavor makes them a great, transportable snack and training treat.

1 banana
½ teaspoon cinnamon

HANDY HINT: *If your pup prefers bigger chews, slice your bananas lengthwise and leave in the oven a bit longer to make longer stick chews.*

1. Preheat oven to 100°C / 210°F. Line a flat baking tray with baking paper.

2. Slice each banana into thin, even chips, and place on lined baking tray.

3. Sprinkle lightly with cinnamon then bake for 1½ hours. Turn your chips and then bake for another 45 minutes.

4. Remove from oven, allow to cool on tray for 10 minutes, and then transfer to cooling racks. Serve.

PUMPKIN PIE CHEW STICKS

―――――――――――――― MAKES 12 PUMPKIN PIE CHEW STICKS. ――――――――――――――

These delectable delights have all the fall flavors in one healthy, chewy snack. The added bonus? Unlike store-bought chews, you know exactly what's in them.

1 cup pure organic applesauce
1 cup pure organic pumpkin puree (not pumpkin pie puree)
½ tablespoon cinnamon

> **HANDY HINT:** *If you'd prefer to make your own applesauce and pumpkin puree, this recipe works just as well with fresh, homemade ingredients.*

1. Preheat oven to 80°C / 175°F. Line a flat baking tray with baking paper.

2. In a medium-sized bowl, add all ingredients and stir well to combine.

3. Using a spoon or palette knife, smear out long lines of the puree on your lined baking tray. The thicker the lines, the longer they will take to dehydrate in the oven.

4. Place in oven and bake for 6–7 hours until your treats are firm and not sticky.

5. Remove from oven, and allow to cool on tray. While they are still warm to touch, cut to your desired treat length and twist into spirals.

On The Grill

While dogs love biscuits and cookies, there's a reason why most dog trainers recommend meat-based dog treats for training.

The strong odor and taste of meat means it gets your dog's attention—and keeps it.

All but one of the recipes in this chapter are made with meat-based proteins, which means they all make effective training treats.

So while you can serve up these burgers, sliders, and pies as nutritious extras on top of your dog's dinner, you'll find using them as training treats will give the greatest reward.

Depending on your dog's size you may have to chop up some of the treats into smaller, bite-sized pieces that make them effective for training—but they'll remain just as tasty and high value.

MINI SHEEPDOG PIES

MAKES 12 MINI SHEEPDOG PIES.

This recipe came about when I was trying to do a spin on a meat-based "doggie cupcake." Alas, when it came time to "ice" my cupcakes, I realized I had unwittingly created mini shepherd's pies. For a healthier version, you can easily replace your topping with sweet potato mash.

4 small potatoes
8 oz. lean ground beef
½ cup whole wheat
    breadcrumbs
1 carrot, finely grated
1 egg
2 teaspoons fresh
    parsley, chopped
    finely

1. Preheat oven to 200°C / 400°F. Lightly grease a mini cupcake pan (12 mini cupcake molds).

2. Peel and quarter potatoes. Add to a large saucepan of boiling water and leave to cook for 15–20 minutes.

3. Combine ground beef breadcrumbs, carrot, and egg in a large bowl and mix with your hands until well combined.

4. Gently roll into 12 small balls and press each into a cupcake well for a smooth cupcake shape.

5. Bake for 15 minutes or until cooked through.

6. While your "pies" are baking, check on your potatoes. When they are tender, remove from heat and drain. Using a potato masher, mash your cooked potatoes.

7. Once your pan is removed from the oven, allow to cool and remove "pies" from cupcake pan. Top with mashed potatoes and sprinkle with fresh parsley.

HANDY HINT: *Depending on your preference, and your dog's health, you can add a small amount of butter and milk to your mashed potato for a smoother consistency, but it is not required. Both butter and milk can upset your dog's stomach due to their high fat content and are generally avoided.*

TURKEY BURGERS

MAKES 6 TURKEY BURGER PATTIES.

These lean meat burgers are great for pups watching their waistline. The addition of zucchini fills out the burger without adding on the pounds.

8 oz. ground turkey
½ cup whole wheat breadcrumbs
1 zucchini, grated
1 egg white
1 tablespoon fresh parsley, chopped finely

1. Combine all ingredients in a large bowl and mix with your hands until well combined.

2. Form into 6 even patties.

3. Cook over grill or in lightly oiled frying pan on medium heat for approximately 8 minutes (or until cooked through), turning once.

PARSLEY: *Just like us, dogs benefit from the breath freshening properties of parsley. As an added bonus, it also is a great source of antioxidants, Vitamins C, K, B, and iron. Doggie kisses, anyone?*

PUPPER FRIES

———————————— MAKES 1 SERVING OF PUPPER FRIES ————————————

These pup-friendly fries will have your dog drooling for days. Baked, not fried, with a touch of fresh herbs, you cannot get a tastier snack.

1 small sweet potato
2 tablespoons coconut oil
2 teaspoons rosemary

HANDY HINT: *These Pupper Fries are best served warm and don't store well. So why not share with your pup? (You can add a dash of salt to yours for extra taste.) They go perfectly with our dog-friendly Mint Dip (page 157).*

1. Preheat oven to 200°C / 400°F. Line a flat baking tray with baking paper.

2. Peel your sweet potato and cut into uniform sticks (resembling fries).

3. Melt your coconut oil over a low heat on the stove.

4. Add sweet potato sticks, rosemary, and coconut oil to a bowl and toss until sticks are thoroughly coated.

5. Place on lined baking tray, and bake for 30 minutes or until golden brown. Remove from oven and serve warm.

DOGGIE SLIDERS

———— MAKES APPROXIMATELY 20–25 DOGGIE SLIDERS. ————

You know how parents pack their kids meals with secret vegetables? Well say hello to the doggie version! These sliders are filled to the brim with nourishing goodness, but taste like a sweet juicy hamburger to your pup.

8 oz. lean ground beef
½ cup cooked organic quinoa
1 small carrot
¼ cup fresh parsley, finely chopped
1 egg, beaten

HANDY HINT: *Your pup will go gaga if you serve these warm! Dip them in our Pupper Hummus (page 158) for an extra special treat.*

1. Preheat oven to 200°C / 400°F. Line a flat baking tray with baking paper.

2. Combine all ingredients in a large bowl and mix thoroughly.

3. Scoop out bite-sized pieces with a spoon and roll into little balls.

4. Place on your prepared tray. Bake for 20 minutes or until cooked through. Serve.

QUINOA: *Packed with protein, studies have reported quinoa is also associated with preventing heart disease and cancer. Makes an excellent rice and grain substitute.*

HEALTHY HIGH VALUE CHICKEN

──────── **MAKES 2 BAGS OF TRAINING TREATS.** ────────

I'm going to be honest, and this "recipe" is so simple it's classified more as "steps" rather than a recipe. But these basic, no frills treats are so simple and quick to make AND they get fantastic results when used in training. The time invested versus payoff make them one of my most valued treats of all time.

2 chicken breasts
2 sprigs fresh thyme

HANDY HINT: *When cutting up your training treats, opt for bite-sized pieces that are just a taste for your dog. When training, you don't want your dog spending a lot of time chewing treats that are too large. You also want to keep treats small as they will consume a lot of them during training and you don't want to overfeed your dog.*

1. Place chicken breasts and sprigs of thyme in a saucepan and pour in enough water to cover.

2. Bring to boil on medium heat and simmer for 10–15 minutes until chicken is cooked through and no longer pink.

3. Remove chicken from saucepan, allow to cool, then chop into small bite-sized pieces.

CHICKEN: *A non-fatty meat, chicken gives a large helping of protein without the high calories. This can assist in building lean muscle mass in dogs and supporting overall general wellbeing.*

KANGAROO TRAINING TREATS

MAKES APPROXIMATELY 25 KANGAROO TRAINING TREATS.

I'll admit it, as an Australian it sometimes feels a bit weird including our beloved kangaroo in a recipe. However, ethically sourced kangaroo is an extremely healthy protein for dogs. I tend to make these treats on the smaller side and then, once cooked, cut into quarters so they are the perfect bite-sized treat for training.

4 oz. ground kangaroo meat
½ cup cooked organic quinoa
1 egg, beaten
¼ cup whole wheat breadcrumbs
1 tablespoon fresh parsley, chopped finely

HANDY HINT: *While kangaroo is a new protein for many, its strong odor and taste makes it an excellent high-value training treat for dogs. Don't have access to Kangaroo? Beef or venison makes a great alternative.*

1. Preheat oven to 200°C / 400°F. Line a flat baking tray with baking paper.

2. Combine all ingredients in a large bowl and mix thoroughly.

3. Scoop out bite-sized pieces with a spoon and roll into small, treat-sized balls.

4. Place on the lined baking tray. Bake for 15 minutes or until cooked through. Serve.

KANGAROO: *High in protein, low in fat, and packed with omega-3's, kangaroo meat helps support a healthy skin and coat, as well as a strong immune system in dogs.*

CHICKEN POPPERS

—— MAKES APPROXIMATELY 20 CHICKEN POPPERS, DEPENDENT ON CHICKEN BREAST SIZE. ——

Once your dog pops, she won't stop! These yummy poppers can be served hot or cold and make for excellent high-value training treats. If you've got a new command or trick for your dog to learn, these Chicken Poppers will get results.

½ cup whole wheat breadcrumbs
2 teaspoons fresh parsley, chopped finely
1 egg
1 chicken breast

HANDY HINT: *You can pop (get it?) your Chicken Poppers in the freezer to save for later. When ready to use, defrost safely and serve.*

1. Preheat oven to 200°C / 400°F. Line a flat baking tray with baking paper.

2. Mix together breadcrumbs and parsley in a medium-sized bowl. Set aside.

3. In a separate small bowl, beat egg with a fork. Set aside.

4. Slice chicken into small bite-sized pieces.

5. Dip nuggets into the beaten egg and then coat with the breadcrumb and parsley mixture.

6. Place the coated poppers on lined baking tray, and bake for 25 minutes, turning once.

7. Remove from oven, allow to cool on tray for 10 minutes, and serve warm.

Special Occasion

There is no better time than the holidays to get in some treat-baking action!

Whether it's some fun Valentine's-themed biscuits, Gingerbread Men during the holidays, or a special cake to celebrate a birthday or Gotcha Day—these treats are the ones that show our dogs just how much they're part of the family.

By making them something special for Thanksgiving or Christmas, we're including them in our celebrations and know we're pampering them in one of their favorite ways—food!

Time to celebrate our puppers.

GOTCHA DAY CELEBRATION CAKE

───────── MAKES ONE GOTCHA DAY CAKE. ─────────

A Gotcha Day—the day of adoption, when a dog officially becomes part of your family—is such a special event on any dog owner's calendar and this cake celebrates it with the love and fanfare it deserves. Here's to all the rescue pups and may they enjoy many Gotcha Days for years to come.

1 carrot, peeled and sliced
1 cup almond flour
2 eggs
1 small handful of berries of
    your choice: raspberries,
    blackberries, blueberries,
    strawberries

1. Preheat oven to 175°C / 345°F. Thoroughly grease and line a 4-inch round cake pan.

2. Place the carrot pieces in a food processor and process until finely chopped. Add the almond flour and eggs, and process until well combined, scraping down the sides of the bowl as needed.

3. Gently fold your berries into the batter, and spoon the mixture into the greased cake tin.

4. Bake for 25–30 minutes or until a skewer comes out clean.

5. Allow cake to cool in pan for 5 minutes and then transfer to cooling racks.

6. Once your cake is completely cool, slice horizontally into 2–3 even parts. Using our Pup-Friendly Cream Cheese Frosting (page 154), frost each layer generously and then stack the next layer. Repeat with all of the cake layers.

7. Using a spatula, apply a thin coat of frosting to the exterior of the entire cake to create the "naked" look. Add any dog-safe decorations.

HANDY HINT: *Swap the yogurt drops for carob drops, and the strawberries for raspberries, for variation.*

VALENTINE'S PUPPY KISSES

———————— MAKES APPROXIMATELY 50–60 PUPPY KISSES. ————————

Say "I Woof You" with this healthy, sweet treat. I love to bake a batch these for February 14th and give them out as puppy Valentines.

5 large fresh strawberries
7 oz. plain yogurt drops

1. Line a flat baking tray with baking paper.

2. Hull strawberries and cut into quarters.

3. Place strawberries in blender or food processor and pulse until they form a puree.

4. Combine the yogurt drops and strawberry mixture in a heat-safe bowl.

5. Melt the mixture over boiling water, stirring constantly as it melts.

6. Once melted, allow to cool for 2 minutes and place into a piping bag.

7. Pipe onto lined tray.

8. Freeze for 45 minutes or until solid.

STRAWBERRIES: *Studies have found strawberries contain anti-inflammatory properties that help relieve pain associated with the inflammation of muscles and joints.*

MOLASSES: *Blackstrap molasses is one of the "healthier" sweeteners for dog treats and contains a number of valuable vitamins and minerals. That said, it is still a sugar and should always be consumed in moderation.*

X'S AND O'S COOKIES

— MAKES APPROXIMATELY 80 SMALL TREATS, DEPENDING ON THE SIZE OF COOKIE CUTTER. —

These fun little doggie hugs and kisses biscuits are a great gift for your doggo friends and make a sweet snack for your pup at home.

Cookie:
1 cup water
¼ cup olive oil
½ cup blackstrap molasses
2 tablespoons honey
3 cups whole wheat flour
1 tablespoon cinnamon

Icing:
10 oz. natural carob drops or plain yogurt drops

X and O cookie cutters required.

1. Get two large bowls. In one bowl combine the water, olive oil, molasses, and honey. In the second bowl combine the flour and cinnamon.

2. Fold the dry ingredients into the wet. Mix until all are combined.

3. Divide the dough into two, wrap each in plastic wrap, and refrigerate for at least 3½ hours.

4. Once chilled, remove dough from fridge and roll out each ball to ¼-inch thickness.

5. Preheat oven to 180°C / 350°F. Line 2 flat cookie sheets with baking paper.

6. Use your X and O cookie cutters to cut out the treats. Place on baking tray. Bake for 10–15 minutes. Place on a baking rack to cool, then ice.

7. To make your icing, place yogurt or carob drops in a heat-safe bowl. Melt the drops over boiling water, stirring constantly.

8. Dip the cookies into the melted drops and allow to cool before serving.

CRANBERRY HEARTS

— MAKES APPROXIMATELY 20 CRANBERRY HEARTS. —

These cranberry cookies delight dogs of all shapes and sizes. While technically they can be made at any time of the year, I prefer to crack out the heart-shaped cookie cutter and make them especially for V-Day.

1½ cups almond flour
1 tablespoon coconut oil
½ cup dried cranberries
2 eggs, beaten
3–4 tablespoons
   coconut flour

1. Preheat oven to 165°C / 325°F. Line a flat cookie sheet with baking paper.

2. Combine your almond flour, coconut oil, and dried cranberries together in a bowl.

3. Once combined, pour in the eggs and mix together with your hands. The dough will be very wet.

4. Begin adding in your coconut flour one tablespoon at a time, mixing in after each addition. You want to achieve a consistency that is easy to roll and not super sticky. This will require between 3 and 4 tablespoons, depending on your brand of flour and size of your eggs. The dough should easily form a ball.

5. Roll out your dough and cut out the treats using bite-sized cookie cutters. Hearts are perfect for Valentine's Day!

6. Place your treats on lined cookie sheet. Bake in the oven for 15–18 minutes or until crisp. Place on a baking rack to cool, then serve.

HANDY HINT: *Sprinkle a little coconut flour on top of your dough to keep it from sticking to the cookie cutters.*

ST. PATRICK'S DAY CUPCAKES

——————— MAKES APPROXIMATELY 12 MINI ST. PATRICK'S DAY CUPCAKES. ———————

The cupcakes are super fluffy for dog cakes. The higher egg volume and leavening agent allows these mini cupcakes to be lighter than most canine cake recipes, but also means your dog's servings should be limited to just 1–2 per day.

½ cup coconut flour
½ teaspoon baking soda
3 eggs
2 tablespoons coconut oil
2 tablespoons organic yogurt
5 basil leaves, finely chopped

> **BASIL:** *An easy herb to grow in your garden, basil has anti-inflammatory and anti-bacterial properties which promote gut, joint, and cardiovascular health in dogs.*

1. Preheat oven to 175°C / 345°F. Lightly grease a mini cupcake pan (12 mini cupcake molds).

2. With an electric mixer, combine coconut flour, baking soda, eggs, coconut oil, and yogurt on low speed. Once combined, mix on medium speed for 2 minutes.

3. Stir basil gently into mixture with a spoon until evenly distributed.

4. Gently spoon the mixture into the greased mini cupcake pan. When spooning the mixture into the mini cupcake pan, gently roll into small balls and press into the tin for a smooth cupcake shape. You want your mixture to fill halfway up with room to rise.

5. Bake for 12–15 minutes or until cupcakes spring back lightly when touched in the center.

6. Remove from oven, allow to cool in pan for 5 minutes, and then transfer to cooling racks.

7. When completely cooled, ice your cupcakes with Pup-Friendly Cream Cheese Frosting (page 154).

HANDY HINT: *Swap the peanut butter for fresh blueberries for variation.*

BUTTER BLISS EASTER EGGS

——————— MAKES APPROXIMATELY 20 MINI EASTER EGGS. ———————

With their sweet carob outer shell and gooey peanut butter insides, these are no average Easter eggs. They're the perfect way to include your pup in the Easter fun.

10 oz. natural carob drops
¼ cup organic peanut butter

Mini Easter egg mold required.

1. Place half of your carob drops in a heat-safe bowl.

2. Melt the drops over boiling water, stirring constantly as they melt.

3. Using a teaspoon, fill each Easter egg half mold evenly. Your carob should fill approximately 20 molds, dependent on your egg mold size.

4. Scoop out bite-sized pieces of peanut butter with a spoon and roll into little balls about half a thumbnail size. Place one peanut butter ball in the middle of the melted carob on each mold.

5. Refrigerate for approximately 20 minutes or until set. When set, the egg halves should easily slide out of the mold. Set aside.

6. Repeat steps 1–3 with remaining carob. (Note: Do not add more peanut butter to the second set.)

7. Place a solid egg half on top of each filled mold so when set, the two halves will be joined. Refrigerate until set. Gently remove the solid eggs from the mold and serve.

HANDY HINT: *To make your Mini Whoopie Pies even "scarier" insert two carob drops into the top of your Whoopie Pie to make a monster face. Boo!*

HALLOWEEN MINI WHOOPIE PIES

──────── **MAKES APPROXIMATELY 15 MINI WHOOPIE PIES.** ────────

This BOO-tiful treat is easily the best way to apologize to your dog for whatever humiliating costume you forced them into this Halloween. Time to get baking...

───────────────────────────────

1 cup peeled, diced fresh pumpkin
1½ cups rice flour
1 tablespoon cinnamon
½ teaspoon baking soda
½ tablespoon freshly ground ginger
1 egg
1 cup honey
1 cup vegetable oil

1. Preheat oven to 175°C / 345°F. Line a flat cookie sheet with baking paper.

2. Place pumpkin cubes in a saucepan, adding just enough water to cover. Bring to boil, cover, then lower heat and simmer for 10 minutes or until softened.

3. Drain pumpkin and allow to cool. Puree in blender or food processor. Chill in refrigerator.

4. Combine flour, cinnamon, baking soda, and ginger in bowl and mix well.

5. Separately, combine egg, honey, and vegetable oil in large bowl and whisk until well combined.

6. Add the chilled pumpkin puree to the wet ingredients and whisk until well combined.

7. Slowly add the dry ingredients to the wet, whisking well until all ingredients are combined.

8. With a teaspoon, spoon the batter onto the lined cookie sheet, spacing about one inch apart.

9. Bake for 15 minutes. To test, insert a toothpick into the cake. If it comes out clean, the cake is ready and can be removed from the oven.

10. Place cakes on a baking rack to cool completely.

11. To make Whoopie Pies, use two cakes and Pup-Friendly Cream Cheese Frosting (page 154) to create a sandwich effect. Serve.

HARVEST MUFFINS

——————— MAKES 12 MUFFINS. ———————

A pup-friendly addition to your Thanksgiving table, these muffins are choc-full of fresh produce and yummy goodness. And with only 4 steps to follow, they're easier than ever.

3 cups almond flour
1½ teaspoons cinnamon
1 cup diced fresh apple, cored & seeds
   removed
1 cup diced carrot
2 tablespoons honey
3 eggs
2 tablespoons coconut oil

1. Preheat oven to 175°C / 345°F. Lightly grease and line a 12-muffin pan.

2. Combine all ingredients and mix in a blender until smooth.

3. Pour batter into designated muffin cups, about ¾ of the way full.

4. Bake for 15–20 minutes. Allow muffins to cool, and serve.

HANDY HINT: *This recipe is very versatile. To switch it up, try it as a cake or use donut molds for a fancy snack.*

HANDY HINT: *Once the biscuits are cooled you can decorate with drizzled carob, melted yogurt drops, or our Peanut Butter Glaze (page 154) if desired.*

GINGERBREAD MEN

MAKES APPROXIMATELY 20 GINGERBREAD MEN.

Festive cheer for your "Naughty or Nice" Pup! These dog-friendly gingerbread men are an all-time favorite holiday tradition in our house and the most perfect treat to end a year on.

3 cups whole wheat flour
½ teaspoon cinnamon
½ teaspoon ground cloves
1 tablespoon fresh ginger, finely chopped
1¼ cups water, separated
¼ cup olive oil
½ cup molasses
2 tablespoons honey

1. Preheat oven to 180°C / 350°F. Line a flat cookie sheet with baking paper.

2. Get two large bowls. In one bowl combine the flour, cinnamon, cloves, and ginger.

3. In the second bowl combine ¾ cup water, olive oil, molasses, and honey.

4. Fold the dry ingredients into the wet. Mix until all are combined. Slowly add the remaining ½ cup of water until the mixture forms a non-sticky dough. Discard remaining water.

5. Divide the dough into two, wrap each half in plastic wrap, and refrigerate for at least 3½ hours.

6. Once chilled, remove dough from refrigerator and roll out to ¼-inch thickness.

7. Use a gingerbread cookie cutter to cut out the biscuits. Place on your lined baking sheet. Bake for 10–15 minutes or until golden.

8. Place on a baking rack to cool, then serve.

GINGER: *Studies have shown fresh ginger has been known to reduce inflammation and upset stomachs in dogs, making it a great ingredient for dogs with allergies.*

HANDY HINT: *If your dough mixture is too wet, add more coconut flour. If too dry, add a little more water.*

"PUPPERMINT" HOLIDAY DOG COOKIES

MAKES APPROXIMATELY 20 "PUPPERMINT" HOLIDAY DOG COOKIES.

Is that Christmas carols I hear? Is that a peppermint-blend latte you have? It's time to break out the "Puppermint" Holiday Dog Cookies! This easy recipe makes the perfect stocking stuffer for all your doggie friends.

2 cups almond flour
4 tablespoons coconut flour
1 tablespoon coconut oil
¾ cup water
4 tablespoons finely chopped fresh mint

1. Preheat oven to 175°C / 345°F. Line a flat cookie sheet with baking paper.

2. Combine all ingredients together in a bowl and mix until you form a ball of dough.

3. Split your dough into two sections. Roll each half of dough into a ball and place on a sheet of baking paper. Slightly flatten the dough and place another sheet of baking paper on top. Then roll your dough to around ¼-inch thickness.

4. Repeat for the second section of dough, place both sections of rolled dough on a cutting board, and leave in the fridge for 20 minutes. This chills the dough, making it less sticky and easier to cut designs that hold their shape.

5. Remove your dough from fridge and cut out the cookies using your favorite holiday cookie cutters.

6. Place your treats on lined cookie sheet. Bake in the oven for 15 minutes, flip, and bake for a further 15 minutes. For chewier cookies remove immediately from oven. For crispier ones, leave in the cooling oven for 5–10 minutes or until they reach your desired level of crunchiness!

7. Place on a baking rack to cool, then serve.

HANDY HINT: *Use a large spoon to drizzle the frosting over the cake. Start heavy in the center and let gravity work its magic!*

HAPPY BIRTHDAY CAKE

─────── MAKES 2–3 MINI CAKE LAYERS TO FORM ONE CAKE. ───────

This very berry cake recipe was developed by Pretty Fluffy writer, Sarah Dickerson, for her dog Coco's fifth birthday. Since then we've had readers from around the globe make this exact recipe for their dog's birthday, allowing their pups to celebrate in style. Now your dog can too.

2 tablespoons
    coconut oil
1¾ cups almond flour
2 tablespoons honey
3 eggs
5 small fresh
    strawberries, hulled
    and diced

1. Preheat oven 175°C / 345°F. Use coconut oil to grease two small ramekin dishes. Depending on the size of your dishes, you may have enough batter for 3 layers.

2. Mix flour, honey, and eggs in the blender until a smooth batter forms, then fold in the diced strawberries.

3. Pour batter into the prepared ramekin dishes, about ¾ of the way full.

4. Bake for 15–20 minutes or until golden brown and a skewer comes out clean.

5. Allow cakes to cool in pan for 5 minutes and then transfer to cooling racks.

6. While your mini cakes are cooling, prepare your Healthy PB Frosting (page 157).

7. Once your cakes are completely cool, spread your icing onto the tops of each layer and stack. Garnish with berries of your choice, and serve.

EGGS: *Contain vitamins and minerals that support brain function, memory, and healthy eyesight.*

Icing & Dips

The perfect finishing touch or accompaniment to the recipes in this book, these icings and dips are as easy to make as they are tasty to eat.

PUP-FRIENDLY CREAM CHEESE FROSTING

———— MAKES ENOUGH FROSTING FOR 6 REGULAR CUPCAKES. ————

This dog-friendly cream cheese frosting is a great option for icing cakes or filling treats that require a fluffier, buttercream-like frosting. For more generous frosting or to ice our Gotcha Day Celebration Cake (page 131), double the recipe.

8 oz. cream cheese (softened)
2 teaspoons honey

1. Combine cream cheese and honey in a bowl and mix until smooth and fluffy.

2. Use immediately or store in an airtight container in the fridge for up to 2 days.

> **HANDY HINT:** *Use pet-safe natural food coloring to change the color of your icing.*

PEANUT BUTTER GLAZE

———— MAKES ENOUGH GLAZE FOR 6 DONUTS OR 12 REGULAR BISCUITS. ————

This thick, gooey glaze is so decadent, it's almost a treat in itself! It's great on doggie donuts, biscuits, and as a yummy filling to make your treats that bit extra.

½ cup organic peanut butter
1 tablespoon coconut oil
1 teaspoon pure maple syrup

1. Melt the peanut butter, coconut oil, and maple syrup in a small heat-safe bowl over boiling water, stirring constantly.

2. Use immediately by drizzling or piping onto donuts, or dipping biscuits.

"CHOCOLATE" ICING

──────── MAKES ENOUGH ICING FOR 12 MINI CUPCAKES. ────────

These pet-safe ingredients make this a great replacement for chocolate icing.

½ cup plain organic yogurt
2 tablespoons organic peanut butter
1 tablespoon carob powder

1. Combine all ingredients in a bowl and mix until smooth and fluffy.

2. Use immediately or store in an airtight container in the fridge for up to 2 days.

> **HANDY HINT:** *Like most dog-friendly icings, this mixture is softer than icings made for humans, so doesn't harden like buttercream versions. Popping frosted treats in the refrigerator usually helps dog-safe icings hold their shape.*

DOGGIE ROYAL ICING

──────── MAKES ENOUGH ICING TO DRIZZLE/DIP 12 BISCUITS. ────────
TO FULLY COVER COOKIES WITH PIPED ICING, DOUBLE THE RECIPE.

Like its namesake, this icing goes on smooth but dries hard for a smooth, shiny finish. It's great for decorating biscuits and special occasion cookies.

½ cup plain yogurt drops
1 tablespoon coconut oil

1. Melt the yogurt drops and coconut oil in a small heat-safe bowl over boiling water, stirring constantly.

2. Use immediately by drizzling or piping onto cookies, or dipping biscuits.

> **HANDY HINT:** *For a "chocolate" version, simply swap your yogurt drops for carob drops. If you'd like to color your icing, use dog-safe food coloring.*

HEALTHY PB FROSTING

———————————— MAKES ENOUGH ICING FOR ONE CAKE. ————————————

This healthy, yogurt-based frosting matches perfectly with our "Happy Birthday Cake" (Page 151).
Serve alongside mixed berries for a tasty flavor combination.

½ cup plain organic yogurt
3 tablespoons organic peanut butter

1. Combine all ingredients in a bowl and mix until smooth.

2. Use immediately or store in an airtight container in the fridge for up to 2 days.

> **HANDY HINT:** *Less stiff than traditional frostings, this frosting works perfectly as a "drizzled" icing over cakes.*

MINT DIP

———————————— MAKES ONE SERVING. ————————————

This simple and fresh dip is a great addition to warmer treats, such as our Pupper Fries (page 121)
and Chicken Poppers (page 127).

½ cup plain organic yogurt
1 tablespoon fresh mint, finely chopped

1. Add your fresh mint to your yogurt and stir through to combine.

> **HANDY HINT:** *No mint? This recipe works just as well with basil or parsley.*

PUPPER HUMMUS

---------- MAKES ONE SERVING. ----------

This yummy hummus is packed with nourishing goodness. It works well as a side to our warm dog treat recipes, but also can be great as a stand-alone filler for Kongs.

½ cup canned or cooked chickpeas
1 tablespoon olive oil
1 teaspoon fresh parsley, finely chopped

1. Combine chickpeas and olive oil in a food processor and process until combined.

2. Place mixture in a bowl and top with fresh parsley.

HANDY HINT: *Beware of human recipes for hummus. They contain garlic, which is a toxic food for dogs. Stick to our pet-friendly version instead.*

THANK YOU

First and foremost, I need to thank my Pretty Fluffy partner in crime, Sarah Dickerson. Sarah has contributed to Pretty Fluffy for so long I can't even imagine the site without her. Her additional recipe development, design work, and photography within this book showcase her flair for creativity, style, and perfection. Sarah—your friendship and support mean the world to me, and your talent blows me away every day. Looking forward to our friendship into the Golden Girl years!

Thank you to the whole team at Skyhorse Publishing for approaching me about expanding our stable of recipes into a book. A special mention must go to Emily Shields for reaching out to me, and of course a huge thank you to my editor, Leah Zarra, for guiding me through the publishing process and helping make the book what it is today. Thank you all for your hard work in making this book a reality.

To my friend, the talented Alex of alexandermayesphotography.com (@alexandermayesphoto), thank you for your stunning photography on the cover and throughout the book openers. Your unlimited enthusiasm and creativity is truly appreciated.

To our doggie models—Ollie (@ollieriver), Akela (@akelablues), Peaches (@badgal_peaches), Buddi (@buddi.the.mini.dachshund), Reggie (@reggietheshepherd), Glory (@anaky_samoyeds) and Coco (@chicsprinkles)—you were all absolute superstars and I can't thank you enough for being part of the book. A special thank you too, to the lovely Dr. Katrina Warren for connecting me with some of our furry models—you're a gem!

Writing a dog treat recipe book is only half the challenge; making sure all the recipes are safe, healthy, and dog-friendly is a big part of the publishing process. Thanks to the wonderful Dr. Leigh Davidson, BVSc, BApplSc (www.yourvetonline.com) for ensuring all the dog treat recipes not only are tasty but vet-approved too!

I'd be remiss not to mention those who have helped me navigate the world of publishing my first book—big thanks to authors Katrina Roe and Sarah Ayoub, whose professional advice allowed me to get my bearings early on. A special shout-out to cookbook author Tessa Sam, whose video tutorial for getting perfect cookies every time (the secret is to pop your rolled dough in the fridge!), allowed me to adapt this method for baking dog biscuits.

To my family, who have put up with me taking over the kitchen for months and months, watching only the dog get fed. To my husband, thank you for being my constant sounding board, photography assistant, and biggest fan. Thank you from the bottom of my heart for your support, and for believing in me. To my darling girl, Emmy—I love you and love making treats with you.

And finally, to all our Pretty Fluffy readers and supporters who have stood proud as crazy dog mamas (and dads!). Without you, this book wouldn't even exist.

INDEX